History of Lady Jane Grey

Also from Westphalia Press
westphaliapress.org

History of
Lady Jane Grey

The Nine Day Queen

by Arthur MacArthur

WESTPHALIA PRESS
An imprint of Policy Studies Organization

Westphalia Press
An imprint of Policy Studies Organization
1527 New Hampshire Ave., NW
Washington, D.C. 20036
info@ipsonet.org

ISBN-13: 978-1-63391-282-3
ISBN-10: 1-63391-282-5

Cover design by Taillefer Long at Illuminated Stories:
www.illuminatedstories.com

Daniel Gutierrez-Sandoval, Executive Director
PSO and Westphalia Press

Updated material and comments on this edition
can be found at the Westphalia Press website:
www.westphaliapress.org

HISTORY

OF

LADY JANE GREY

BY

ARTHUR MAC ARTHUR, LL.D.

OF

WASHINGTON, D. C.

Author of " Education in its Relation to Manual Industry,"
" Biography of the English Language," etc.

———————

1896.
GLENS FALLS PRINTING CO.,
GLENS FALLS, N. Y.

CONTENTS.

CHAPTER I.

CHAPTER II.

CHAPTER III.

CHAPTER IV.

CHAPTER V.

CHAPTER VI.

CHAPTER I.

War of the Roses.   Houses of York and Lancaster.   Their Claims
to the Crown.   Destructive Nature of the War.   Henry VII.
His Marriage to Elizabeth of York.   Their issue.   Henry VIII.
Edward VI.   Ancestors of Lady Jane Grey.   Mary Stuart, the
First Ruler of her sex upon the Island.   Lady Jane Grey
Exscinded from the Record of English Royalty.   The Dying
Choice of Edward.   The First Queen Regnant over England.
Her Execution.   Two of Henry. VIII.'s Consorts Beheaded.
Margaret of Salisbury also Beheaded.   Remarks of Lingard
and Mackintosh.   Diana de Poitiers.   Universal Grief.   Her
Death Condemned as a Crime.   Marquis of Dorset, her Father.
His Ancestry.   Her Birth in the Year 1537 at Bradgate.   The
Greys had Already Furnished a Queen of England.   Henry
VII. not the Legal Heir, Genealogy Considered.   Henry
(VIII.) becomes Affianced to his Brother's Widow.   Details of
this Episode.   He Finally Believed the Marriage Incestuous.
Anne Boleyn, Mother of Elizabeth.   Will of Edward VI.   Con-
veying the Crown to Jane Grey.   Crowned Queen.   Henry
VIII.'s Will.   Brilliant Prospects of her Reign.   Mary Tudor.

CHAPTER I.

T the outbreak in 1455 of the calamitous war between the House of Lancaster and the House of York, the emblem of the first was a red rose, and of the other a white one. The point upon which the pretensions of these two great factions turned was mainly the usual one of primogeniture. The Yorkists claimed the throne in favor of a hereditary right in the royal branch they pronounced the elder one, and to which they adhered. The Lancasterians similarly vindicated their assumption and insisted as firmly upon prescriptive and indefeasible succession. In addition, they possessed the sanction of a parliamentary settlement of the crown. The partisans of both roses had at their command arguments derived from statutory enactments and from the deadly crimes committed on either side. The War of the Roses had not spent its force until

the destruction of nearly all the princes of the blood had narrowed down the succession to Henry, Duke of Richmond, fancifully described by Shakespeare as vanquishing Richard III. on the field of Bosworth. Indeed, Philippe de Comines, who was perhaps the most credible historian of those times, informs us that no fewer than sixty or eighty princes of the blood-royal of England lost their lives in this quarrel, either in battle or on the scaffold, and that all the nobles of the Lancasterian party were either killed in battle or executed, or had fled into foreign countries to save their lives. The nobility were threatened with extir-pation, and the depopulation of the country was only too visible in the ruined towns and cities and in the uncultivated fields and decaying trade of the whole people.

After the Battle of Bosworth Field, Henry, Duke of Richmond, ascended the throne as Henry VII., and his marriage to the Lady Elizabeth, daughter of Edward IV., merged the claims of the two houses, and might be considered as much a Lancasterian triumph as a matrimonial coalition of rival interests, that had been so long destructive to society. Their issue was Henry VIII., from whom the crown passed to his only son, Edward VI., a mere boy of nine years. In his seventeenth year he left a vacant throne and a testamentary devise of his crown to the Lady Jane Grey.

The eldest sister of Henry VIII., named Margaret, married the King of Scotland, and thus became the grandmother of Mary Queen of Scots, and his other sister, Mary, became the Queen of Louis XII. of France, and after his death the wife of Charles Brandon, an English nobleman of large estate and remarkably attractive in person and manner. Their issue was a daughter, who in turn became the mother of Lady Jane Grey. It will thus be seen that she as well as Mary of Scotland was in the collateral line of succession to the English throne, a circumstance that cost both of them their heads.

We can easily recall the name of each Queen who has held the British sceptre by right of birth alone. The first hereditary ruler of her sex upon that island was Mary Stuart, and the last Victoria, who reigns today by virtue of her origin from that ill-starred Scottish princess.

In passing, it may also be observed that the omission of the name of Jane Grey from the catalogue of British monarchs is a remarkable instance of the way in which the facts of history are so often suppressed or artfully veiled from their just place in a truthful narrative. She was the brightest ornament of her sex and century, and ascended the throne of her ancestors under the sanction and concurrence of every authority within the realm, and yet the books which chronicle the races and accessions of English royalty exscind from the record this personage of princely blood and next in succession to a king of her lineage; one whose birth was indisputably legitimate, all her English co-heirs having been bastardized by church and state, and even by their own father, Henry VIII. She was also the dying choice of Edward, his son, for he bequeathed his throne and power from a death-bed to the gifted, chaste, and lovely Lady Jane Grey, scion and representative of all that was pure in the blood of Lancaster. Sir Bernard Burke, in his book of titled people in the United Kingdom of Great Britain and Ireland, called *Burke's Peerage*, passes with the mutest silence over the proclamation, coronation, and the whole reign of the most gracious and innocent young being whose brow was ever circumfused by the arched diadem of England. He observes that she was beheaded, and in that remark is comprised the whole peerage and history of the first Queen regnant over England, Ireland, and Wales, to whom the highest nobility in the land had knelt and

sworn allegiance. But her's was not the only crowned
head that had suffered decapitation to gratify the ferocious passions of those in power. Henry VIII. set
the example by executing two of his six consorts, and
his daughters, Mary and Elizabeth, afterward followed
that example by sending their cousins, Jane Grey and
Mary Stuart, to the headsman's block. Of these four
sovereigns, all, both murderers and murdered, were or
were to be Queens regnant, each receiving the sceptre
in her proper person. But Henry had accustomed
the world to look upon his sanguinary deeds with a
habitual and almost apathetic horror, which rose to its
climax when the last of the Plantagenets, Margaret,
Countess of Salisbury, memorable from extreme age
and beloved for the conspicuous virtues of her long life,
was brought before the executioner, and, refusing to
bow her head to his ax, was dragged by her gray hair
to the block, where, as the old account says, she was
"manglingly butchered." She had committed no
crime, but was condemned unheard, simply because
Henry hated her son, Cardinal Pole.

That dreadful era in which virtue seemed the
surest path to destruction has left to our unspeakable
sympathies the names of these matchless daughters of
misfortune. The Catholic historian of Mary Tudor's

reign exclaims: "Far better would it have been for her name and honor had she turned her hand from that foul deed." And Sir James Mackintosh, one of the most enlightened writers of this century, in speaking of the execution of Jane Grey, laments this cruel sacrifice by saying: "The example is the more affecting as it is that of a person who exhibited a matchless union of youth and beauty, with genius and learning, with virtue and purity, whose affections were so warm, while her passions were perfectly subdued." Her execution caused a profound emotion, but terror suppressed the universal grief, and there was a cry of horror in all the courts of Europe except that of Spain, whose King had urged the bloody sacrifice through his Ambassador at London. Diana de Poitiers wrote to Mary Stuart as follows: "Madame, they bring to me the account of the poor young Queen Jane, and I cannot but weep at the sweet and resigned language that she uttered on the scaffold. Was there ever a more accomplished princess?" France, Germany, and Switzerland condemned it as a crime, and such it has been pronounced by posterity, and while the memory of Jane Grey is tenderly cherished, that of Mary Tudor lies in the sepulchre of ages, more inexorable than her own obstinacy, and it can be whitened by no partiality, nor its blood-stained record softened by the hand of time.

Henry Grey, the Marquis of Dorset, resided on his estate in Leicestershire at the time of the birth of Jane Grey, which occurred in the year 1537. Her father's ancestry dated anterior to the Conquest and was of French origin. The family name of Grey came from the lands and chateau of Cory in Picardy, from which sprang the name of Grey. They all had large possessions, and held many conspicuous positions under the Government. In royal ceremonies they held high rank. At the coronation of the Queens of Henry VIII., her grandfather had been created Duke of Suffolk for his services at the Battle of Pinkie, and he had also the honor of carrying the sword of state at the interview between Henry and the French monarch, Francis I., at the famous Field of the Cloth of Gold. Her father was the third Marquis of Dorset, and came to the title in 1530. He was Constable of England and possessed other high trusts under the Government. Besides this, the Greys had furnished one Queen to England, for the mother of Elizabeth of York and of the unfortunate princes immolated in the Tower of London by Richard was a Lady Grey, widow of one of the Lords of that name, and who after his death

married Edward IV., and thus by the marriage of her
daughter to Henry VII. the line of the Tudor dynasty
was rendered legitimate, for that monarch was not the
heir of the house of Lancaster, at least not the legal
heir.   He was only the grandson of an illegitimate son
of John of Gaunt, Duke of Lancaster.   The Tudor line
stood much in need of being reformed.   The red rose
was not pure upon the diadem of Henry VII., and
this is why, notwithstanding his victory at Bosworth,
he lost no time in marrying, on the 8th of January, at
Westminster, Elizabeth of York, upon whose white
rose there was no blemish.

Let us look at the case again, for it is the most
singular one, genealogically considered, in all history.

Henry VIII. had two sisters, two daughters, and
one son.   Margaret Tudor was the eldest of the sisters, and next to her in lineal descent stood her grand-
daughter Mary, the celebrated Queen of Scotland.
Next to her in succession came the representative of
Mary Tudor, Margaret's youngest sister, once married
to the King of France and after his death to Charles
Brandon ; their daughter became the mother of Lady
Jane Grey.   It will therefore be seen that the Lady
Jane and Mary Stuart were second cousins to each
other, having Henry VIII. for their grand-uncle, but

that the Scottish princess was of the elder branch of the collateral inheritance, and first entitled to the royal succession to the English throne.

The two daughters of Henry were Mary, the child of the faithful and ever blameless Catherine of Aragon, who was divorced by him because he thought they were committing adultery together, she having been the widow of his brother, who died before he came to the crown, and because he thought the marriage was denounced by Leviticus. This question was supposed to have been settled eighteen years before, at the time of their engagement. I pause for a moment to glance at this singular little episode.

Henry VII. had two sons, the eldest being Prince Arthur, and the other Henry, who succeeded him. Arthur married Catherine of Aragon, and after living with her four months was seized with an illness of which he died. Before long Henry developed a strange and overruling passion for his brother's widow, and with that overwhelming impetuosity which belonged to his character he became affianced to her in spite of all opposition and against the religious scruples of the age. But Henry VII., his father, took occasion to declare that the nuptials would be incestuous as violating the law of God inscribed in

Leviticus, "Thou shalt not espouse thy brother's wife"; and Warham, who was the Primate of England, was of the same opinion, but Fox, another Bishop of almost equal authority, in order to please the Prince gave a contrary opinion, and Pope Julius II. promulgated a Bull sanctioning the contract. But notwithstanding the Bull and the acquiescence of the Bishops therein, the reasons were so strong against the proposed espousal, that the conscience of Henry VII. continued to be very much troubled, and acting under the stings of remorse, on the 23d day of June, 1505, when his son had reached his thirteenth year, he constrained him, at the Palace of Richmond, to protest against the marriage. The good faith of this protest is open to suspicion, for it was made in private and strictly concealed from Catherine and her friends, nor was the slightest intimation of it communicated to the Spanish Ambassador. It was a secret. Whether this performance relieved the scruples of the King or not, it planted in the changeable mind of his son some dangerous ideas, for after having lived with his brother's widow in great conjugal peace and happiness for about eighteen years, he then began to entertain the most serious doubts concerning the legality of his marriage, and after studying the subject and consult-

ing the most learned men in his dominions he pro-
fessed to believe that his marriage was incestuous and
against the law of God and nature.

We know that on the death of his father he was
crowned King of England as Henry VIII. The
Ambassador of Ferdinand then demanded the immediate fulfillment of the union between him and the
Princess Catherine. Warham renewed his objections,
but Fox replied that the Pope had already decided
that matter when the contract of marriage was entered
into five years before, and that it was not for an
English Minister to invalidate a Roman Bull. The
Council voted the marriage, and it was celebrated on
the 11th of June, 1509, at Greenwich, in the royal
palace, with great pomp and splendor.

Having mentioned Mary as one of the daughters
of Henry VIII., we return to the other, who was Elizabeth, the offspring of the ill-fated Anne Boleyn,
whom he beheaded because he thought she was committing adultery without any participation on his
part. The only son of Henry and the gentle Jane
Seymour, his third wife, succeeded to his father, and
died after a peaceful reign of nine years as Edward
VI., making a settlement of the crown in his will on
Lady Jane Grey, his cousin, to whom he was devot-

edly attached. By an unparalleled defect of male competitors for the sceptre of England, these rival women, all of royal blood, contended for the crown of William the Conqueror.

We have seen that the will of Edward VI. conveyed the crown directly to Jane Grey, and within a few days it was solemnly placed upon her head, and for a period of ten days she was the Queen of England. We know by extant records, backed by the concurrent assent of all history, that in the thirty-fifth year of Henry VIII. a statute was passed empowering him to settle the succession by his last will. This will is yet preserved in the charter house of Westminster Abbey, and on all hands acknowledged to be genuine. Now what does it ordain? It directly entails the crown upon the heirs of his youngest sister, Mary, in preference to those of his oldest sister, Margaret, by marriage dowager Queen of Scotland, to be inherited after his son Edward, his two daughters, and their issue; which, however, failed in all of them, they dying without heirs. What was the operation of this will as affecting Jane Grey? His son, Edward VI., was dead childless. If the arguments adduced against the lawful capacity of Mary and Elizabeth are sound, and their brother Edward pronounced them cogently so in

excluding them by his will, Lady Jane being the
eldest heir of the preferred family, was incontestably
the next in succession, and rightfully crowned and
anointed a queen.   Besides all this, Edward bequeathed
her immediate possession of the sceptre and sword, and
in excluding his half-sisters, he did by them exactly
what his father did by his own sister Margaret.
Thus the violence and caprice of her grand-uncle,
Henry VIII., had prepared a passage under her feet to
the throne, built of tears and sorrows, and the dying
commands of his son directed the nation to conduct
her safely over it.   It seemed as if the shades of
departed kings had conspired for her elevation.   Absorbed in the enjoyments and in the discharge of the
amenities and duties that engrossed the private life of
a noble matron, she was torn from her graceful pursuits and the singularly elevating studies in which
she delighted and was proficient, to administer the
government over a people as tempestuous as the ocean
that encircled their home; and no doubt visions rose
before her mind of those tragic disasters that had
befallen the dynasty to which she had become heir,
and of the murdered hosts that overshadowed her
inheritance.

No greater misfortune could have happened to the

country than her removal from the government. At
that time there were flattering omens that the oppres-
sive spirit of feudality was about to disappear.   Prac-
tices that had lingered were growing obsolete if not
extinct.   A better fortune seemed as if about to crown
an era of new intelligence and energy, for the Renaissance had found the shores of England, and learning
was reviving.   All semblances foreboded that the
name of Jane Grey would be identified with long and
peaceful advances in humanity; that it would be
blended with the renewed vestiges of science, commerce, and discovery; that the bond of society would
be softened and ameliorated by an intellectual reign,
in which learning and polished intercourse would find
her their patron and directress.   Indeed, we cannot
overrate this keystone period between the dark ages
and the time of our own birth.   But these prospects
were immediately overcast in gloom and disappointment by her removal from power and the accession of
Mary Tudor to her place upon the throne.   Instead of
the gentle and benign spirit of Lady Jane Grey, the
former was cold, distrustful, and hypochondriacal by
temperament, and followed the sternest councils that
expediency whispered; widely unlike her father, she
was never moved by passion or caprice, but appears to

have examined every measure before decisively acting upon it. Unfortunately, in spite of her undoubted and various talents, her principles and opinions upon sovereign power over the conscience and religious belief of her subjects were unsound to the core. A right judgment upon this single point would have lifted from her memory a mountain of obloquy, and her short reign would not have been detested in the inverse proportion to its brevity. To the judgment of this austere occupant of the throne, circumstances had consigned the life or death of the pure and guileless heroine she had just deposed.

CHAPTER II.

CHAPTER II.

T was at her father's residence, situated about four miles from Leicester, that the birth of Jane Grey took place. It was a noble old baronial mansion in the midst of a great park, with a forest near by several miles in extent, used by the family and their guests for the chase, as was usual in all the dwellings of the feudal nobility. From the period when she graduated from the nursery, she had the attendance and train of a princess, consisting of governesses, preceptors, and numerous servants. Dr. John Aylmer, who was afterwards created Bishop of London, by Elizabeth, made frequent visits to Jane. He was, of all the friends who surrounded either her infancy or her adolescence, the man whom she most admired and who had the most influence over her. He was gracious and gentle, of an exalted and mystic soul, a genius at once keen and sagacious, and with a profound erudi-

tion, and he added to all these gifts a kind and
affectionate address, that secured the love and admiration of his pupil.   She was, indeed, the pupil of his
choice and heart.   Jane was always delighted with his
presence and she valued nothing so much as a walk
or a conversation with the good Aylmer.   One visit
of his to Bradgate, which was the local name of her
residence, was hailed with delight, and a visit of some
weeks was sufficient to direct her studies for several
months.   She remembered his instructions and con-
formed to his counsels.

It was in the imposing forest on the estate of her
father—that forest which had belonged to the Kings
of England before and after the Conquest; the forest
in which Richard Cœur de Lion had struck down
the wild boar; where Henry VIII. had killed the
fallow deer—that Jane often came to study or medi-
tate.   Here seated upon the downy mosses with
Aylmer, they would converse either upon theology,
philosophy, or fate, under the mysterious obscurity of
the oaks.   At the age of nine years she astonished
Aylmer and all her masters, and we read even now
with surprise of her uncommon intelligence, docility,
and beauty.   She did not believe, as did the vassals of
her father, that Cardinal Wolsey came forth in the

nighttime, from his tomb in the Abbey of Leicester, riding upon his mule through the woods of Charn-wood. But in her admiration of classical paganism she was inspired with the mythological legends of the Renaissance, and the dim forest appeared to her imag-ination full of oracles. But the greatest spirit that animated her was the spirit of Christianity, and it was this thought that lifted this youthful soul to visions of the infinite. She had periods of religious fervor that filled her with the ecstasy of heavenly rapture. The forest of Charnwood, which was only a hunting ground for the Marquis of Dorset, was a world of poesy and prayer to his daughter Jane Grey. Perhaps the princess, who, according to her years and circum-stances, was attentive only to her studies in language, history, the Reformation, and the tragedies of Grecian literature, had still, in addition thereto, caught a glimpse in her calm retreat in the County of Leicester of that chaste love so sweet to virgins. Perhaps! It is justifiable to conjecture that we have not overdrawn what were the impressions of Jane Grey in the leafy shadows of Charnwood. These contemplations were natural to a mind whose passions were literature, the elegant arts, and equally full of sensitive and feminine tenderness. Sir Roger Ascham, tutor to the Princess

Elizabeth, tells us that having one day paid her a visit he found her engaged in reading Plato, while the rest of the family were engaged in hunting in the forest; on his admiring the singularity of her choice, she told him that she received more pleasure from that author than from any gaiety. Remarkable as such an acquirement would be even at this day in a young woman, it was but one of the intellectual accomplishments by which she was distinguished; she knew Latin as familiarly as Queen Bess herself, who was constantly taking up her Bishops for false quantities and slip-shod prosody.

On another occasion in the summer of 1550, there was a distinguished company at Bradgate. A hunt in the vast forest of Charnwood had been arranged. The hunters were all ready for the sport. The house was filled with a joyous tumult. The horses were saddled and harnessed, neighing and pawing the ground in the court-yards. At the moment of starting the company perceived the absence of Jane Grey. "Where is she?" they asked each other after having vainly sought for her. Her two little sisters declared she was in the park. Upon this the whole party began a search for the traces of the beautiful Jane. They rushed about on the gravelled paths and found her under a willow tree at the edge of the water, surrounded with young deer, and leaning over her favorite Plato, in which she was absorbed and on which rested the curls of her hair. At the noise, she rose upon the grass and returned thanks to her friends for their courtesy. She closed the dialogues, while blushing, and gave the book in charge to one of her attendants. She then joined the horses and galloped with her friends through the shades of the forest to the clanging hoof and sound of the hunting horn. She was, of course, reprimanded by her mother, the imperious Duchess of Suffolk.

In those olden times almost every sylvan retreat was lighted up with some legendary tale. Charnwood had more than one of these charming incidents which were rehearsed around the fireside, as there were no books or newspapers to beguile the time in the long evenings. One of these legends related to her grandfather, the Marquis of Dorset, according to which he had gone forth into the woods with a grand hunting party to pursue the stag. On his return he had outstripped all his companions, and was resting in an open space where he had hidden a stag in the thicket, and was sitting on his horse enjoying the cool, humid air of the approaching evening. Suddenly he beheld a knight whom he did not know coming at full speed upon one of the routes that converged upon the open space, and he stopped only when at a lance's length from the Marquis. The stranger knight then addressed him, saying:

"My Lord, you have upon your domain the most beautiful young woman in Great Britain, one of your vassals. She has resisted many allurements, some say from chastity, and others that it is from love of your Grace. I am of this last opinion, but whatever it may be, I saw her this week at the Fair of Leicester, and whether you love her or not, I forewarn you that I wish to make her my mistress."

"Before that," cries the Marquis, "I shall have dug thy grave in this forest. Thou liest in thy throat in attacking this young woman! Upon my honor she is as prudent as beautiful. It is not me, but one of my archers whom she loves." While uttering these words the Marquis prepared to draw his sword and attack the stranger knight. "Saint George!" he cried, sinking his spurs in the flanks of his horse, but his horse moved not, nor would his sword come forth from the scabbard. By this time the Marquis saw approaching another knight, who rushed upon the stranger and felled him to the earth with a fiery blow.

The prostrated knight did not rise again but dissipated into cinders, and vanished in smoke and sulphur. "By heaven, who are you?" asked the Marquis. "I am Saint George, the Patron of England, and the protector of thy home," replied the Saint. "My son, I came at thy invocation. This man whom I have overthrown is Satan himself. He tempted thee. He sought to excite thy passions for one of thy vassals. She is so honest and true that she merits all thy kindness." And with these words the Saint disappeared.

The Marquis went home in a dreamy abstraction, that did not leave him all night, and as soon as it was daybreak he sprang from his bed and proceeded at once to the dwelling of the young woman, and spoke to her about her preference for a husband. She confessed, while blushing, that it was himself. The Marquis smoothed away all the difficulties to such a match, and endowed the beautiful virgin of Bradgate with an ample dowery. They became husband and wife within the year.

Jane Grey did not invoke Saint George for assistance. She believed alone in God and her Saviour.

It is perhaps hard for us to believe that a beautiful and interesting girl, yet in her teens, would be employed in the perusal of Plato, and deriving from it more gratification than from sports and occupations which are congenial almost universally with the bounding spirits of youth; and we naturally think that something more than simple, unbiassed inclination is necessary to account for it, and yet the story is in strict conformity with history. We owe the 'story of her virtues and accomplishments to sources which have described without exaggerating them. The impression of her character, so full of tender and lofty sentiments, is perhaps the only secret which marks her conduct at this period and forms the connecting link between her youth and her genius. But if an additional motive were wanting for her choice of occupation, it is supplied by an extract from Roger Ascham's "Schoolmaster," by which it appears that her parents contrived to make her so thoroughly wretched while she was otherwise engaged, that it was no wonder she should find recreation in Greek. The passage is as follows:

"After saluation and duetie done, with some other talke, I asked her why she would leese such pastime in the parke? Smiling she answered: 'I wisse all their sport in the parke is but a shadow to that pleasure I finde in Plato: alas! good folke, they never felt what true pleasure meant.' 'And how came you, Madame,' quoth I, 'to this deepe knowledge of pleasure, and what did chiefly allure you to it, seeing not many women, but very fewe men have attayned thereunto?' 'I will tell you,' quoth she, 'and tell you a troth, which perchance ye will marvel at. One of the greatest benefites that ever God gave me, is that he sent me so sharpe and severe parents, and so gentle a schoolmaster; for when I am in presence either of father or mother, whether I speake, keeper silence, sit, stand, or go, eate, drinke, be merry, or sad, be sowing, dauncing, or doing any thing else, I must do it as it were, in such weight, measure, and number, even so perfectly as God made the world—or else I am so sharply taunted, so cruelly threatened, yea presently sometimes with pinches, nippes and other waies which I will not name, for the honour I beare them, so without measure misordered, that I think myself in hell, till tyme come that I must go to Mr. Elmer, who teacheth me so gently, so pleasantly, with such faire allurements to learning, that I think all the time whiles I am with him as nothing.—And when I am called from him, I fall on weeping, because whatsoever I do else, but learning, is full of greefe, trouble, feare, and whole misliking unto mee: and thus my booke hath been so much my pleasure, and bringeth dayly to me more pleasure, and more, that in respect of it, all other pleasures, in very deede, be but trifles and troubles unto mee.'"

This curious narrative gives its just and fair proportions to the character of this extraordinary woman, and softens the extravagance of that peculiarity so marked in her studies. A girl of seventeen with all the advantages of beauty, rank, and wealth voluntarily giving herself up to the study of Plato and the philosophy of the Dialogues, is a spectacle that excites our surprise, if not our admiration. It astonished

Ascham that one so young should know so much of
those sublime truths, which were then almost a secret
to all but a very few of the best scholars, and yet
nothing can be more interesting than to see that she
could resort to these studies as a retreat from the
tyranny and persecution of her parents.   Says the
historian of a later date: "The cultivation of the
female mind was hailed by the wise, the good, and
noble of England as a proof of the increasing refinement of the land."   In later centuries invidious igno-
rance has almost succeeded in flinging a word of vulgar
opprobrium upon such women as blue-stockings.
There were other ladies of the Court, as well as several
who did not belong to the Court, who were celebrated
for their love of letters and their ardor in the pursuit
of knowledge.   In the first rank are the daughters of
the Duke of Somerset, the Lord Protector of the kingdom under Edward VI., and Mildred Cecil, daughter
of Lord Burleigh, as well as the wife of the latter;
Margaret Roper, the matchless daughter of Sir Thomas
More, and her child, who recalled the intellectual gifts
of her mother; Catherine Parr, the sixth and last wife
of Henry VIII., and Queen Elizabeth belonged to the
same brilliant company of thoughtfulness and learning.
Sir Thomas More, Erasmus, and Ascham all but dei-

fied these women, and yet they would all be inevitably stigmatized today with the opprobrious epithet if they had lived in the 19th instead of the 16th century. Ascham has celebrated them all, especially Elizabeth and Jane Grey; but it was the latter who, in his opinion, surpassed all the others by her intelligence.

Jane Grey and her family were Protestants. Great masses of the people, as well as of the gentry and nobility, had adopted the new faith and the new learning, the first having been introduced by the Reformation, and the latter by the Renaissance, and both were greatly helped by the growing intelligence of the people. The age was advancing. New light was flowing in upon mankind. As early as 1477 Earl Rivers and William Caxton were the first English writers who had the pleasure of seeing their works published from the printing press; but in the time of Jane Grey it had multiplied books and made them accessible to all classes. By this means knowledge was much more general than in former times, and an opportunity was presented by which persons of different opinions could communicate their views to the public. A great number of small books on religious subjects were published, and many were imported and translated into English. Even those of Luther and Wickliffe, although prohibited by church and state, were secretly circulated and read with great avidity by the people. Indeed, the religious idea had taken a powerful hold upon all classes, and the free discussion of the rights of conscience had roused the agitation of religious thought. A great change had taken place in the feelings of the people toward the church and its exorbitant power. The corruptions, the rapacity, the pomp and pride of the priesthood, had been a standing theme of satire from the days of Langland and Chaucer, and a growing desire for a better state of things was manifested in many ways. Not the least of these was the revival of the ancient learning, and many scholars came over from the Continent to spread its beams. Most of the leaders of the Reform movement were men of great learning, and they had not only introduced the reading and study of the Scriptures, but of the languages in which they were originally written.

In fact, all over Europe the prevalence of reform ideas had been visible to all observant minds, and the force of the change had been felt in every city and town, and in every home and individual conscience. The great church which had dominated modern nations so long became the object of critical comment,

and its dogmas were reëxamined by some of the
master minds of the age. The upheaval was general
and partook of the character of a revolt. The first
great schism was in England, where the authority of
the Pope was denied and the Catholic Church was
entirely subverted. The same thing was observable
in many parts of the Continent, especially in Germany
and Switzerland; but the propagators of the reform
encountered the terrors of persecution, and many of
them took refuge in England. At the period of which
we speak—that of Jane Grey—it was the only place of
safety open to them. They found here not only
friends who welcomed them, but positions at once
honorable and useful. Bucer, who had reformed the
Church of Cologne, was invited by Archbishop
Cranmer to England, and was installed at Cambridge
in the chair of theology, where he died in 1551, and
was buried with great pomp; but five years afterward,
in the reign of Mary, his body was dug up and burned.
Here also came Pierre Martyr Vermigli, a man of prodigious learning and bold, uncompromising convictions; he had preached all through Italy, France,
Germany, and elsewhere, in danger of the poniard
and ready for the dungeon or the stake. He was settled at Oxford in the chair of eloquence and rhetoric.

· III.

One Sunday his friends, as well as his enemies, wished
to dissuade him from expressing his views about the
Lord's Supper. This was because he denied the Real·
Presence in the eucharist, and they showed him the
hostile multitudes that filled the streets. "What matters it," he exclaimed, "to me, who have not feared
the Inquisition? I do not fear the people"; and he
spoke as fearlessly as if he had been surrounded by his
supporters. Colet, though maintaining his connec-
tions with the Church of Rome, preached such liberal
and radical doctrines at St. Paul's, that his clerical
brethren accused him of rank heresy. Erasmus often
visited England, and spent much of his time at the
Universities, where he was held in high esteem for his
immense learning.

The motive which appeared to govern the reformers was the preservation of pure religion and the
right of private judgment. The Scriptures were
regarded as the source of all faith and doctrine, and
the diffusion and reading of the Bible became a cardinal point in their reformation. The men who have
just been mentioned were familiar with the languages
of Europe, the Italian, the French, the German, and
others, while the Latin, the Greek, and the Hebrew
were studied with renewed ardor and shed a halo

of refinement and philosophy over their efforts.

Nothing delighted Jane more than to listen to the discussions of these learned men, in which she sometimes joined in an easy, chatty way, that pleased the auditors, and they were struck with her modesty as well as astonished at the wisdom of her conversation. The Dialogues of Plato became to her almost a sacred book. It was the Phaedo that Sir Roger Ascham found her perusing during his visit at Bradgate, already described; and this circumstance gives us the measure of her faculties and her sentiments. It is the argument for the immortality of the soul. This is the central idea of God in the human conscience.

The Phaedo describes the last interview of Socrates with his friends. He had been condemned to die, and his sentence was to be executed that evening, and they had assembled to hear his last words. The dialogue was suggested by the circumstances and naturally turned upon death and immortality. The arguments in favor of a future life are set forth with Socratic terseness and splendor. The existence of the soul is assumed, and we are told that he who lives as a true philosopher has reason to be of good cheer when he is about to die, and that after death he may hope to obtain the greatest good in the world. "But I am confident," says Socrates, "that there is truly such a thing as living again, and that the living spring from the dead, and that the souls of the good are in existence, and that the good souls have a better portion than the evil." He enforced his views by arguments drawn from the doctrine of ideas which exist in the mind, and which can be received only from the objects or things external to the senses. The idea of immortality is one of the highest of these impressions, but how came it into the mind if there was nothing to produce it? The objects of sense appeal to our respective organs; those of sight, of touch, or of color produce their appropriate ideas and command our belief. Why should not the consciousness be treated with the same confidence that we bestow upon the outward senses, and should not its formal abstractions become the basis of confidence and belief? His doctrine that recollection is knowledge, is also pressed into the evidence, and from hence he derives his fantastic belief that the soul remembers the knowledge it has gained in a previous state of existence, and as it lived before birth it is sure to exist after death. But the great argument is drawn from the goodness of God and the consciousness of life in the soul itself.

From these wonderful dialogues it appears that the

ancients had many ideas that are still the subjects of
inquiry.   There were those, then as now, who were
obstinate in maintaining that the things only which
can be touched and handled have any existence, and
the materialists of the 19th century do not appear to
have moved a peg out of the ancient scepticism.
While some of the philosophers accepted the idea of
immortality, others were as far from that belief as are
pantheistic writers of our own times.   The doctrine
of transmigration, advocated by Pythagoras and believed
in by Plato, is reproduced by the reincarnationists of
theosophy; and the theory of the Ionic school, which
undertook to solve, by means of a single primordial
principle, the vague problem of the origin and consti-
tution of the universe as a whole, finds a close counterpart in the school of modern evolution; the idealism
of Berkeley and Hegel, which holds there is no external
world, and that all the objects which we think we see
are mere subjective ideas generated in the brain, and
having no more materiality than color to the eye,
sound to the ear, touch to the skin, odor to the nose,
or taste to the mouth; and that the universe has no
existence except in relation to the mind, which merges
all these impressions into the subjective idea; a mere
lesion of the brain, an image painted on the retina.

There is, therefore, no cosmos except that which exists in the mind, like the baseless fabric of a dream. All this is not without a shadowy resemblance to the obscure notions of the sophists, who held that the transitory nature of all things might be represented as a passing shadow, that left little or no impression of a form or lasting character. Plato believed that ideas and sentiments which are invisible constituted what he termed the divine essence or soul, and today we have an analogous mysticism revealed in the ambitious speculations of Kant and other German philosophers. Says Sir Dugald Stewart: "There is a choice erudition, penetrated throughout with a peculiar vein of sobered and subdued Platonism, from whence some German systems, which have attracted no small notice in our own times, will be found, when stripped of their deep neological disguise, to have borrowed their most valuable materials."

It may surprise us that so young a person as Jane Grey could find pleasure and instruction in the light thus thrown upon the most minute parts of our metaphysical conceptions, and understood them so well that her preceptors were continually astonished by her intelligence and knowledge.

But a new career was opening for society in which

there should be a fuller recognition of human rights, and in which manners and institutions should take on a grander conception of spiritual relations. Many of these thoughts had already taken possession of individual consciousness. Martin Luther had emancipated the intellect, and henceforth in all matters of a speculative character the utmost freedom of inquiry was to be observed. Francis Bacon, before the end of the century, was evolving his method of inductive philosophy and showing science itself how to investigate and reach the truth; and soon afterwards the celestial wonders of space were to be penetrated by the not less wonderful telescope and astronomy placed upon an unerring basis. The moment itself was auspicious. The Western Continent had risen from a geographical problem to one with the united world. Printing, the great colleague of speech, presented its wings to intelligence. Fire-arms bestowed the control of almost a new elemental power; and the feudal chain that bound men to the caste of birth was breaking link by link throughout the land.

The world was apparently hastening on to newer and higher conditions. The inspirations of the times were therefore profoundly elevating to those who read and reflected. To Jane Grey we may be sure they had a deep significance. One penetrated by such lofty ideals, and who to all the attractions of her own sex united a degree of learning rare even in the other, could not but feel the enthusiasm likely to be created by these noble harbingers of the future. I do not wish to detract from the merits of the contemporaries of Jane Grey, but it is quite possible that she had her own perceptions of the tendencies of the age, for she could estimate the worth of a movement by her deep religious convictions. She knew that the past for centuries had been weighed down by heavy burdens of cruelty, superstition, and oppression, and had been wholly without the means of progress; and she also knew that her Plato, restored from the mould and occult receptacles of the dark ages, informed her of the marvelous learning of the Greeks in philosophy and literature, and that their knowledge of the human mind, as shown in the metaphysics of Socrates and the dialectics of Plato, had never since been equalled. She was also aware that the hopes of mankind had been renewed by the discovery of these treasures of knowledge, and that the glorious race who were the authors of such systems of thought were still teaching lessons in the sublime and beautiful that would elevate modern life as they had refined that of the ancient days.

The hymn of the Oracle, and the sacred song of the Pythian rhymes lived again, and the Greek genius and the Greek evangelical morality respired in the pages of the Phaedo, breathing the eternity of God and the indestructibility of man. This is the last word of the Greek philosophy and it is the first one of the Renaissance.

In the beginning of English history we have an example of how great things may flow from small ones. The English people were not a very important part in the world till several centuries after the rise of other nations, like that of Italy and France. But the ground had been broken, the seed had been planted of a new empire, which should reach out its dominion far beyond the confines of the then civilized world. The great strides of English influence and power have given it the control of the most populous regions of the earth and the richest as well as the most ancient empires. No one can contemplate the history of this wonderful people without being struck with their energy and character. Not alone in the conquest of its arms, not alone in the conquest of its commerce, but in the spread of its language, its literature, and its principles of government, it has furnished an example without a parallel in modern times.

Beginning with a band of sea kings and pirates, they, driving out the native populations and establishing a kingdom of usurpers, seated their own princes on the throne and required all the provinces to pay tribute to their own, and grew into a compact and formidable nationality, which for several centuries held sway over the whole southern portion of the island. At length they experienced the same fate which they had imposed upon the original inhabitants, and fell before the victorious cohorts of another invader, who extinguished their ancient laws and divided their lands among his followers. William the Conqueror took possession of his new kingdom as if he had purchased an estate, and robbed the owner out of all compensation for his booty. We now behold a bold attempt to transform a nation by dint of military vassalage, and to maintain it by force and the semblance of law. The experiment succeeded by the power of organization, for no system was ever better calculated to secure a given purpose than the establishment of the feudal law and its remorseless enforcement upon a vanquished people. But order grew out of disorder. Peace and prosperity sprang from war and oppression, like Cæsar from the knife. The inborn principles of human nature asserted themselves from time to time. The King was taught some wholesome lessons by the people, and the nobles often found their interests the same as the commonalty. There were periods of fierce war. The nation was convulsed with contending factions and civil strife. At length Parliament asserted its power in matters of peace and war, and assembled in order to deliberate upon the common welfare. Courts of Justice were established to determine private controversies without resort to arms. The common people rose gradually into the controlling element of the commonwealth, and public opinion louder than the thunder of armaments was heard with reverence and obeyed with respect. Our mother tongue became the language of all classes; it had been broken into dialects that spurned all grammar, and had disappeared in fusion with the classic models that formed the English of our own day; so graceful in the march of its periods, so full of its cadences upon the ear, so rich in images and so condensed in sentences, so grave and noble in diction. So little is there of vulgarity in its idiomatic freedom and racy combinations, that it may well be doubted if any other spoken tongue unites the capacities of our language or can produce passages worthy of comparison; while to the great luminaries and master spirits of the later centuries is due the refinement and polish of our literature, our philosophy, and poetry, which have taken a front rank in modern civilization.

But what has all this to do with Jane Grey? The life of a nation depends upon a great variety of circumstances, and the condition of individuals is determined by their environment. Had Jane Grey been born at a much earlier period of English history, her own history would have been very different. She was like most others, the product of her age, and, therefore, affords a fine historical example of English growth and maturity. If it be true that the character and condition of women is an index of the civilization and culture of the age and country, then, indeed, we have in such women as she an instance of all that there then was or had been in the great race to which she belonged.

It was evident to the clear intelligence of Jane Grey that more depended upon the individual himself than upon any other influence. She therefore cultivated the highest intuitions of the mind and stored it with knowledge. She read the classics, as they were the only books that circulated, and she pondered the maxims of antiquity as well as the learning of her own times, in order to be ready for whatever might befall her. She corresponded with learned men upon the Continent, and had the advantage of their wisdom and advice. She was fully conscious that to one in her position it was necessary that she should be educated all round, and not in any particular branch alone. Her studies therefore embraced the modern languages as well as the ancient ones, and a general knowledge of history and diplomacy. She was well versed in the correspondence of English and foreign ambassadors and the different systems of education in the Courts of Europe. In church history and theology she was particularly well informed, and was also an adept in the writings of the Reformers both at home and abroad. She never stopped to consider whether any of her studies were of special use to her, believing that all knowledge is useful and that the sure test of its utility is in its effect upon the mind. When, therefore, she had no one to direct her studies she would consider whether they would have a salutary effect upon the understanding or upon the feelings. She could read the Greek authors without any fear of being injured by their allusions to the vulgar things in Greek life, for to the pure in mind all things are pure and such persons take no stain from the evil parts any more than the sunbeam does from the mire over which it glances in the streets.

CHAPTER III.

.

47

CHAPTER III.

E will now turn to the period when Jane Grey made her appearance at Court. The personal importance of her father, the Duke of Suffolk, and the relation her mother bore to Henry VIII., as his niece, would have naturally insured her welcome admittance into the royal circle. The King, however, was in his last days. His frame had become so unwieldy that it was moved about the apartments of Westminster Palace only by aid of machines contrived for the purpose; his limbs were so enlarged and bloated up with humors, that his hand refused to sign his name. Stamps were prepared to affix to written instruments instead of his signature. Death soon afterward came to his relief, and certainly to that of all his subjects.

It appears that at the time of Jane Grey's advent into the royal palace, the Queen, who was the sixth and

last of his consorts, was the refined and elegant Catherine Parr, who was charmed and delighted with the
grace and beauty of the young princess.   The youthful
lords were attracted by her loveliness, and the renowned
warriors and statesmen were equally delighted with
her modesty and surprised at the wisdom of her conversation.   It was a new scene in the life of Jane, but
she did not fail to see under all its glitter and ostenta-
tion the bitterness that filled many hearts and the
servility that was evident in all the homage rendered
at the footstool of power and prerogative.

Among the hosts who knelt at the shrine of
patronage none had cultivated their opportunities
more than the brothers of Jane Seymour, the third
wife of the King and mother of the boy destined to
become King Edward VI.   Her inoffensive and irreproachable life, together with the King's unbounded
attachment to her person, enabled her family to rise
like motes in the sunbeam.   The portion of their
career that attaches itself to the immediate history of
Jane Grey is a curious and instructive instance of an
ambitious cabal aiming at the exclusive control of all
the collateral branches of a royal family, and working
it like the veins of a quarry of precious stones.

After Warwick, the kingmaker, celebrated by one

of our greatest novelists as the last of the barons, it is
difficult to find another instance of machinations so
deliberate and comprehensive as those which partly
succeeded aud partly failed in the hands of Edward
and Thomas Seymour. In the first place, they
acquired titles and positions as the King's brothers-
in-law. They were brothers to his wife and uncles to
his son Edward, and the younger brother, Thomas,
after the King's death, effected a marriage with Catherine Parr, Queen dowager and step-mother to this
prince. There were, it is true, facilities in his way
which rather heighten than cloud the picture; for they
had been sweethearts in more humble days, when she
was a widow for the third time, and Lady Latimer
only; but as fortune threw the King in her way she
accepted the sixth reversion of His Majesty's hand, and
in three years and a half death obligingly restored the
former position of affairs in regard to her lover. The
tree near London is still pointed out to romantic tour-
ists where they met to renew their troth whilst the
King's funeral was going on. Nor had the delay and
her wedding to the King been without value. She
brought her patient admirer a brilliant fortune the
King's fondness had enabled her to amass; and so
soon as the possibility of her being the mother of a

posthumous heir to the crown had vanished, they
became man and wife. Their forbearance to this step
extended to thirty days after the death of Henry VIII.
In no love match do we find the elements of prudence
and sentiment more discreetly blended.

It may be said with her contemporaries that the
dowager Parr was a very irreproachable, but a very
marrying widow. Her husband was now created Lord
Sudley and High Admiral of England. He was
accused, however, of poisoning his admirable lady,
which imputation was false; but he was also charged
with making love to the Princess Elizabeth, who
resided with them, which was notoriously true, and,
moreover, this young lady returned his affection with
such an ardor and good will at the age of sixteen, that
her removal was deemed expedient to a separate
household, and was immediately acted upon.

In his lifetime Henry had treated four out of six
of his marriages as absolute nullities, and he spoke as
if he were a widower of the ordinary kind. Here is
his language: "Forasmuch," he says, "as His Majesty
since the death of the late Queen, Jane Seymour, has
taken to wife Catherine Parr"; then between the death
of Jane Seymour and his marriage with Catherine
Parr he seems to have forgotten that he had married

two other women, one a foreign princess, and Catherine Howard, a domestic one, and he goes on with the provisions he was settling without condescending to remember the existence of his daughters, or rather ignoring them as if they were people of a dream, who were out of place in any account of his wedded life. Soon after the death of Anne Boleyn these secluded victims of a living father's cruelty, both motherless and legally orphanized, lived together in sadness and gloom upon a miserable pittance, until the marriage of Catherine Parr. This humane woman, whose memory redeems the supposed harshness of a thousand step-mothers, gathered her step-children of so many mothers under one roof, and by her example and wisdom imbued them with a love for the scholarship they all signally attained. At her suggestion Mary executed the well-known translation of the Gospels from the Latin paraphrase of Erasmus. The respect and affection they all bore this prudent and amiable lady is seen by extant correspondence to have continued to the last moment of her life.

After the accession of Edward VI. Elizabeth remained with the widowed Queen, and they were soon after joined by Jane Grey as a member of the family. In fact, Catherine, although only the King's relict, retained her importance as the only crowned personage in the kingdom, and kept up a retinue and ceremonial of almost regal splendor and expenditure. The presence of Jane Grey as a member of this splendid household was a fortunate event, for here she received the same education as the royal children, and Queen Catherine took the same pains in her training as if she were destined to wear a crown.

The residence of Jane Grey with the dowager Queen was perhaps the happiest period of her life. She had lost the familiar objects of her home at Bradgate and the gloomy shades of the grim old forest, where she had so often wandered and studied, but she had found the banks of the Thames, and instead of the chase, which she disliked, the Queen and Jane would mount their horses, with two or three servants, and visit the surrounding country, going from cottage to cottage, under the gray sky and in the light vapor that veils the landscape in England, and distribute alms to the poor, courtesies to the rich, and Bibles to all, of which the servants always had a supply.

What is known of Catherine Parr develops singular testimonies in her favor, and reveals a constant succession of her goodness and charities, a deep consideration for the unfortunate, and affection for the

little step-children whom she befriended. We also
hear of her kindness to her dependents, and of her
endeavors to promote the welfare of her numerous
godchildren, and of her habitual almsgiving. Among
her many accomplishments was a fondness for horti-
culture, flowers, birds, and music. To these were
united easy affability, winning manners, and a noble
carriage. The praise of personal piety is undoubtedly
due her, and, of the most decorous and exemplary
character herself, she infused into her household the
proprieties and decencies so sadly deficient in the
Court of which she was lately the Queen, but could
not control. Her personal accomplishments could be
advantageously compared with any of the brilliant
women of her age; nor should we forget her wander-
ings to relieve the indigent cotters and worn-out
retainers, with an open hand and a consolatory voice,
that fell upon the objects of her compassion as softly
as the summer breezes they inhaled.

Catherine had many trials with her royal husband.
Not infrequently he would test her soundness on
religious topics, and more than once tried to entangle
her into heretical views. On these occasions Catherine
would raise her sweet voice and entertain as well as
amuse the King. Her ideas had probably some

affinity with those of the sectaries, who preached in
the streets and in private houses ; and Catherine had
openly attended some of their meetings, and no doubt
had imbibed some of the opinions of Anne Askew,
who was the most attractive apostle of hersey in the
kingdom, and both Catherine Parr and the Duchess of
Suffolk, mother of Jane Grey, had been carried away
by her beautiful life of piety and self-sacrifice. She
had been burned at the stake for her heretical
harangues. Lord Gardiner, Bishop of Winchester,
who had the scent of a bloodhound and the remorseless cruelty of an inquisitor, suspected the Queen, and
having a conversation with the King at which she
was present took the opportunity to introduce theo-
logical discussions, in which all three of them excelled,
and Catherine without seeing the trap that had been
set for her disputed some points both with the King
and the Bishop. When she left the apartment the
King after remaining silent for a moment observed to
the Bishop that he was troubled in his conscience
about the views his wife had just expressed, and the
Bishop replied that he was as much so as His Majesty,
and the Queen was upon the borders of heresy. Just
then Wriothesley, the Lord Chancellor, entered the
cabinet, and upon being informed of the views

expressed by the Queen, declared that she was the centre of religious opposition and perhaps of political discontent. "What is to be done?" asked the King. "Confine her for a few weeks in the tower," replied the Chancellor, "and it will teach her to be more circumspect." Henry, in a half-serious mood, directed him to prepare the warrant of imprisonment, which was done on the spot, and he signed it. When Wriothesley took his departure the warrant was left behind and accidentally fell into a corridor of the palace, where it was picked up and carried directly to the Queen. The shock was terrible, for she knew that none of Henry's prisoners ever came out of the portals of that gloomy fortress, except on their way to the scaffold or the stake. She felt all the danger she was in, but resolved to find the means in her own address and mother wit to avert the storm that was about to break upon her head.

In the evening she joined the King. He was afflicted with an ulcerous sore upon his left leg. Indeed, he was bloated and swollen all over his body, and Catherine nursed him herself. The dressing of his leg was a matter of much difficulty, and the Queen usually performed that work with her own dainty fingers, with a touch so soothing upon the afflicted part that the soreness appeared to fly before her gentle ministry. On this evening, while she was busy with her ointments and bandages, the King endeavored to renew the discussion of the morning, but she refused the challenge, and declared that she was already sufficiently enlightened and convinced by his reasoning.

"Man," she said, "was made in the image of God, and woman in the image of man. It is, therefore, her duty to defer to her husband, and I, above all women, owe a particular submission to the wisdom of Your Majesty. Are you not the greatest King and the grandest theologian in the world? You have conquered Francis I., without doubt, but have you not also vanquished Luther and the Pope? Who will dare to maintain with you a serious controversy?" "You, Dr. Cath.," responded the King, much delighted. "No, no," said Catherine, "neither I nor any one else. If I discuss with you it is only to give animation to the conversation; it is only for the purpose of directing your attention from your pains, and to call forth your logic worthy of Saint Thomas, and that I may the better understand the principles which teach and edify me. Ah! Sire, I know all my happiness and good fortune, and I return thanks to God that my duty is to believe in him whom I love and admire so

much." "Is it so, my dear heart?" cried the King
with tenderness, "we are then reconciled," and drawing the Queen into his arms embraced her.

The following day the King was in the gardens
with Catherine, when Wriothesley arrived, prepared to
arrest the Queen and conduct her to the tower. He
left an armed troop outside the entrance. The King,
recalling the matter of the warrant, moved his chair
upon its rollers in front of the Chancellor, and then
ensued a scene fit only for a burlesque opera. "What
do you want?" exclaimed the King, "idiot, triple fool,
unworthy knave! Go to! go to! It is you I will
lodge in the tower." The Chancellor disappeared
immediately, and from that day to this it may be
safely affirmed that no Chancellor of England has ever
been addressed in such infamous language. Catherine,
however, asked the King to pardon him. "Poor
Cath.," said Henry, "speak not to me of that con-
temptible figure. It is not for you to implore my
clemency for this rascal."

Catherine had an exquisite *finesse*. She could
discuss the religious problems of the day with the
subtlety of a theologian, but henceforth she observed
the precautions of a diplomat and the graces and
docility of a woman. She charmed the ferocious

temper of the colossal Tudor who was her husband. She disarmed and ruled him. She had a wonderful attraction for Jane Grey.

No wonder that Jane loved the Queen, for to her she was, indeed, a second mother; she would often converse with her on subjects of the highest character, and smile at the astonishing intelligence of Jane, who passed from natural objects which appeared strange to science itself and asked the names of the planets, the meaning of books, or the sense of words. The energy and grace of her imagination had full scope with the Queen, who encouraged her boldest flights into the regions of the infinite.

Aside from the days set apart for special purposes, it was the habit of the Queen to make excursions with Jane and Elizabeth along the banks of the Thames. Mounted upon their noble steeds and surrounded by a train of illustrious friends and their attendants, they would pass over the meadows and parks that seemed to stretch out to the horizon. The Queen excelled in leading conversation and in giving it a pleasant turn, and Jane often took part in these discourses, to the delight of Catherine. Their promenades in the free air along the river, upon the gravelled tracks and lawns shaded by elms and cedar trees, fascinated Jane;

her health was fortified and her beauty became radiant. The strict discipline which she hated was less severe in the family of Catherine than in that of her father, the Marquis of Dorset, and she revered the Queen dowager's profound erudition and the indefatigable indulgence of Aylmer, her professor and director.

We now approach the period of Jane's historical life, but before trenching upon the subject it may be well to dwell for a moment upon her personal appearance and conduct. Her age was nearly seventeen years. Had we not perused many accounts of persons, not only in early youth, but in absolute childhood, who had mastered such varied knowledge that it almost appears to have been born with them, we might hesitate to rely upon the relations of Jane Grey's extraordinary acquirements. The daughter of Sir Thomas More, Mary Tudor, Jane Seymour, and Somerset's daughters were considered prodigies of feminine learning, but Jane Grey surpassed them all in the depth and variety of her information. There are at this day no doubt many young ladies greater proficients in almost any branch to which she had turned her attention, but when we reflect upon the uncompromising rudeness of the time, her birth, and position, and duties, we must agree with the dispatches of the French Ambassador to his Court, in which, dwelling upon the phenomena of such youth and learning together, he says that "she was wise in worldly matters, virtuous, and beautiful."   In the extant pictures of her person we observe that conformation of forehead that almost speaks for itself, and is the unfailing index of capacity in woman.   Were it not relieved by large liquid eyes, that seem to look upon you with retreating glances, the intellectual stamp and force of her brow would be almost masculine.   Her features were not of the Tudor or hard Plantagenet type, then unextinct in their descendants. They are said to have been the counterpart of her wondrously beautiful aunt, Eleanor Clifford, whose mother, after having been Queen of France, lost her heart for a second time to the same paragon of her first love, Charles Brandon, the Adonis of Henry VIII.'s reign.   The pencil of time has mingled a tint of its own with that which Holbein endeavored to catch from the color of her hair, but the harmonious outline and the mould of her features are yet unimpaired on his canvas.   Half tender and half heroic, now sad and anon sparkling with flexibility and animation, the face of Jane Grey was of that magical class which rivets the first glance and requires no second perusal to be remembered forever.   We have verbal

pictures of her contemporaries perhaps more reliable
than the colors. Three hundred years have mellowed
since the great painter of his day transferred her linea-
ments to posterity. They inform us that her com-
plexion did not make a permanent contrast of white
and red, but that without being blonde it had the
transparency unfortunately denied to decided bru-
nettes, and fluctuated from a pale to a crimson only
when excited or animated by a flush of fancy or emotion. Unimpassioned in general, but when delighted
her serious aspect vanished and her dancing eyes were
accompanied by those little smiling concavities called
dimples. This rendered her girlish abandon irresistible. Not above the middle stature, she looked tall.
The setting of her head and the constant observance
of a dignity, partly natural and partly acquired, con-
ferred a prestige that few were apt to set at naught.
She moved with the pace of a young and perfect form.
Its full development had probably not taken place, for
she died before she had attained her full height.

In Latin she carried on a correspondence of the
most extraordinary character with her friends abroad.
It is still read with wonder by the Latin scholar, and
some of her biographers have been led to conjecture
that she must have been aided by her preceptors, so

perfect is her use of that language.   She spoke several
modern languages, Spanish with her cousin Mary, and
French with the French Ambassador.   Italian literature, which had been transplanted into this cooler clime
by the admiration of Chaucer for the "Divina Comedia"
of Dante, was a standard branch of education with the
higher classes of that day, and ranked among the favorite acquirements of the Lady Jane, and she wrote sonnets
in that tongue.   And it is said that, aided by the learned
men who praised her astonishing acquirements as an
honor to letters, she kept up with the progress that
oriental literature was then making in England; and
although so young she had neglected none of the outdoor
exercises beneficial to her own sex.   Nor should we
forget her love for the country and her enjoyment of
every beauty the pencil of nature delineates, nor her
wandering through the woods, the lanes, and wild flowers with attendants, like herself in almost rustic attire,
relieving the indigent and encouraging the worthy
and the deserving.   Nor had she overlooked the
lighter accomplishments.   Her performance upon
musical instruments that were fashionable three hundred years ago, when Chickering pianos and Evard's
harps were mute and unstrung, was both dexterous
and pleasing.

Her intuitions breathe a divine harmony. "In departing from evil we approach nearer to God," she said to Catherine Parr.   And to Ascham she confessed, "If the Creator of the heavens and the earth had not revealed Himself by the Scriptures, I believe firmly that I would have found Him all alone"; and to Aylmer she remarked, "If there was no other proof of a Sovereign Being than the firmament, that would be enough for me.   From the stars to our eternal Father there is only a step."

v.

CHAPTER IV.

CHAPTER IV.

THE presence of Lady Jane Grey as a member of the household of Catherine Parr was due to a stroke of Lord Sudley's policy. Both the Seymour brothers, Edward, Duke of Somerset, and Thomas, the Lord Admiral of England, participated in the government of the kingdom. The Duke, who was the elder, was chief of the executors of the King's will and Protector of the realm. The younger, Thomas, the Lord Admiral, was a member of the Council. Both were bent upon similar objects in different ways. The Admiral had the principal support of his Queen wife; the Protector was the superior in office and had access to the royal closet. The variance between the two brothers was stimulated by the female influence exercised in the Protector's family. His wife was a tartar of the first water, and as near a virago as ladies in good society, especially a Duchess,

can be supposed to exist. As her Chancellor says,
"She was a woman of many imperfections, intolerable,
and for pride monstrous." She hated her charming
and fortunate sister-in-law with invincible animosity
for her general superiority, especially in rank. "Marry,
come up!" said she one day to her friends, "did not
Henry VIII. marry that little Kate Parr in his doting
days, when he had sunk himself so low by his debauch,
lust, and cruelty, that no lady who stood upon her
honor would venture upon him, and shall I now give
place to her who in her former estate was only Latimer's widow, and who is now fain to cast herself upon
my husband's younger brother? If Master Admiral
Sudley cannot teach his wife better manners, I am the
one who will do it."

The Duke contemplated among other designs to
bring about a union of his daughter with the youthful
King. For this, and, indeed, for any project whatever, he had ample opportunities and intended to
improve them by every means in his power. In addition to this scheme of matrimony he also cherished
the intention of marrying his son to Lady Jane Grey.
But the dowager Queen had countermined his plan by
giving Jane an education that fitted her in every
respect for a King's wife, and had already warmed

their intercourse into a gentle sentiment, that tended
to result in deeper feelings for each other. When
Sudley became the husband of the dowager Queen a
confidential messenger was sent to Jane's father, the
Duke of Suffolk, with a proposition that they should
enter into a secret arrangement as far as their joint
interests were concerned in certain matters, in opposition to the Protector's intrigues. In a short time the
Duke of Suffolk privately visited the Queen at Sudley
Place, her residence, and entered into full explanations.
The Duke was carried away by the ardor and plausi-
bility of the scheming pair, for so feasible did it
appear with the coöperation of the dowager Queen,
that an *entente cordiale* was ratified with all its details
before the conference closed. This, of course, placed
the pretensions of the Protector's son to the hand of
Jane Grey under somewhat difficult circumstances.
We have evidence that Suffolk surrendered the ward-
ship of his daughters to his associates in this royal
marriage plot for five hundred pounds sterling. The
pecuniary feature of this transaction sounds to modern
ears as more detestable than the usual immoralities of
an age as gross as 1548. But it was an age when both
sexes drank several pints of strong ale at breakfast
and called all kinds of things by their unsophisticated

names.   Had Edward lived and obtained free access to
the dowager's society and household circle, it seems
highly probable that the chances were in favor of his
bestowing his hand upon the lovely companion of his
youth, to whom he entrusted his kingdom in preference to so many other competitors.   But an event of
more than human interposition was at hand to wrest
from Sudley the triumphs he proposed and to baffle
his utmost art and power.   The death of the Queen,
his wife, dissolved the intimate connection and dimin-
ished his facilities for intercourse with the persons
whose fate he was busy in moulding.

The minority of Edward presented a favorable
arena for the political gladiators of the time.   During
the minorities of former sovereigns, powerful conspir-
ators, who were styled protectors, but who would now
meet with the appellation of traitors, ruled nominally
for the sovereign, but actually and substantially made
the sceptre sway in obedience to their own ambition.
Edward was too young to act without the sanction of
the Regency Council, and too old and intelligent not to
have fancies and favorites.   Both his uncles were in
power.   Lord Sudley, the younger of the two, kept up
the close intimacy due to their double relations, but
the power of the elder one, Edward, went on contin-

ually increasing. He received titles as Governor of His Majesty, and Protector of all his realms, and Lieutenant of all his armies. Had the bond of relationship remained unbroken between these powerful and ambitious brothers, they were in a condition to sway the fortunes of the kingdom, but the boundless aims that animated both unfortunately separated their interests, and first neutralizing their power, ultimately destroyed them both.

After the death of his wife the Admiral resumed his intrigues to supplant the Protector and to marry the Princess Mary, although he was a Protestant champion and she the most pronounced Catholic in England. He had also made love to the Princess Elizabeth, upon whom he had impressed a girlish partiality. We know that she was as versatile in her tender fancies as she was warm in entertaining them, and in the 17th year of her age found leisure to listen to the protestations of Lord Sudley's passion, that in maturer years she spared from the pursuits of ambition and power to whisper in bower and corridor with the pliant Robert Dudley. But the Admiral was not destined to take two Queens to his bed. A darkened cloud overspread his horizon and obscured the star under whose beams he had sailed on to fortune. His ambition grew wilder and less circumspect, and his audacity culminated into open defiance of the Protector's government. Desertion and disappointment gathered more closely round his uncurbed and defiant spirit, and as his fortunes became desperate he resorted to open sedition and turbulence. He endeavored to obtain possession of the young King's person, bribed the officers of state, and bought over many of the principal nobility, and failing to excite a rebellion, was brought to trial by his brother and sentenced to death by his nephew. He died as gallantly as he had lived. He boldly proclaimed from the scaffold that he had been condemned treacherously and unjustly. Before he laid his head upon the block, he tried to transmit a letter to each of the princesses who had been the objects of his devices. It is noteworthy that this double courtship of Mary and Elizabeth indisposed either of them from interceding in his behalf. Elizabeth mourned his loss with many bitter tears and sorrows. "He was fierce in courage," says the historian Hayward, "courtly in fashion, in personage stately, in voice magnificent, but somewhat empty in manner." The phraseology in which he bade farewell to the ruling powers has not reached us, but beyond doubt it possessed the virtues of candor and emphasis; and he must have given them some bitter truths as a parting souvenir. It was on the 17th of March, 1549, that he laid his head upon the block—that head beautiful as the head of Antoninus and martial as that of the youthful Hotspur. It was severed at one blow.

Jane Grey now deprived of her best friends left the roof of the Seymours for the second time. It had been to her a charming sanctuary of scholarship and refinement. At Chelsea or Hauworth, which were the residences near London preferred by Catherine Parr, she had met all that was eminent in England for learning and accomplishments. The distinguished foreigners who sought toleration and safety, such as Bucer and Colet, the savants and artists like Holbien, the Germans, Florentines, Venetians, and other Italians who were friends and promoters of the Rénaissance, added a picturesque element to this brilliant circle. The state was represented by its highest dignitaries, the Chancellor Wriothesley, the Protector Somerset, the Marquis of Northampton, brother to the Queen, the Earl of Warwick, father of that Dudley who shall yet be the husband of Jane Grey. The church had also its most eminent divines among the visitors, such as the Archbishop Cranmer, the Primate Bishop Ely,

and Bishop Ridley, the greatest preacher of the new
faith, and many others, besides the young lords and
ladies of the Court, who thought it an honor to be
associated with so much that was noble and illustrious.
These souvenirs will ever be fresh in the tender memory of Jane Grey.

She now spent her time either at Bradgate, or at
the Palace Dorset in London with her father, or at
Hampton Court, and sometimes at Greenwich or
Windsor, near her cousin, Edward VI., who wept with
her over the loss of the great Admiral, whose tragic
sentence he had not dared to set aside or modify.
Other tears, even more bitter than those of Jane and
Edward, were those of Elizabeth. The Admiral had
been the first love of that princess. She suppressed
her lamentations in her solitude at Hatfield. She
remained silent and prudent in the midst of her grief
and surrounded herself with testimonials of Seymour.
She gave one of the positions in her house to Har-
rington, who had been devoted to the Admiral, and who
composed some verses to his memory at the request of
the princess as if they had come bursting from her own
heartstrings. She became more and more attached to
Mistress Ashley and Mistress Parry, who had been the
mediums of communication between her and her lover.

From the day of his execution the commencement of the downfall of the all-powerful Somerset may be dated. He at once confiscated all the property of his brother Sudley into his own possession. He, it is understood, suffered the niece, the child whose birth had cost poor Catherine Parr her life, to vanish in obscurity and poverty. The fate of this unfortunate heiress is unknown. As far as the voice of authentic history can reach us from a period so distracted, it seems as if each rival interest was resolved upon the utter extermination of its opponents. They were inspired by no sentiment in which love of country had a share, or in which any generous feeling was an incentive. All was for the aggrandizement of individual, or classes, and that the mighty power of England might be exercised by the most imbecile or the most inhuman miscreants.

Among the executors of Henry VIII. was John Dudley. He was the son of Edmund Dudley, who had been employed by Henry VII. to extort money from his subjects, but such had been the corruption and excessive oppression practiced by him, that in the early part of Henry VIII.'s reign he was tried for his iniquitous and flagrant infractions of the law and executed amidst the execrations of his victims. John

Dudley, his son, inherited his plunder. Nevertheless, he rose in that capricious monarch's favor and was created the Viscount Lisle and given the command of the fleet in the war with Scotland; he was made the Earl of Warwick by the Regency under Edward VI., February 17, 1547. His fourth son, Lord Guildford, married Lady Jane Grey, and his third son became the celebrated favorite of Elizabeth, and was created by her Earl of Leicester. On one occasion he said to Edward VI., "Your father deprived my father of his life, but I will cheerfully sacrifice my life in your service." Equalling his father in rapine and extortion, and of a far more insatiable ambition than his renowned namesake, the king maker, he fomented the inhuman variances between Edward and Thomas Seymour. The latter being dead he set about procuring the destruction of the survivor. His aim was facilitated by a growing dissatisfaction towards the Protector among the nobility.

It was a period of great suffering, and there were popular uprisings in many parts of the country. Those in the South were the most serious, but Lord Russell put them down by a strong military force, and an ill-concerted outbreak was crushed out by Warwick in the North, and Kett, the peasant leader, was hung.

The Protector extended pardons to many of the insurgents, and this indulgence seemed like complicity to some and like pusillanimity to others. Warwick, whose fame was now at its height, employed his emissaries to spread those and many other evil rumors all over London and in the counties. It was laid to the Protector's charge that he ingratiated himself with the populace to the prejudice of the nobility; that in the late disturbances he had exercised a culpable lenity toward the Rebels; that he systematically disregarded the opinion of his coexecutors, as well as that of the regents, by whose advice it was maintained his public acts should be governed. The odious part he had acted in the destruction of his brother was also brought up against him, and the vast estate he had amassed was attributed to the plunder of royal and ecclesiastic lands. Instances of sacrilege were urged against him for removing churches and Episcopal mansions to furnish a site for Somerset House, the most costly and sumptuous palace that had ever been erected by a subject in the realm, and it was further charged that he used the stones and masonry of the demolished chapels for the construction of the new structure, in which accusation the mutilation of the monuments and effigies of the dead, with the transportation of bones long interred in the church of St. John, of Jerusalem, to unconsecrated ground, was the most obnoxious and abhorrent. No outrage more poignant could be inflicted upon the descendants of warriors who had fought in Palestine and borne the red cross over the field of Ascalon, than the defacement of the escutcheons and recumbent statues of their founders, and the violation of their tombs. Parishes rose in tumult to save their time-honored edifices, and all religious persuasions, being of a common ancestry, vied with each other in reproaching the desecration.

His colleagues in the council who had been restive under Somerset's authority combined to annul it altogether. His degradation was accomplished, and they imposed an enormous fine upon their late master. Emboldened by this success they soon found him guilty of aiming at the life of Warwick, and by invoking the aid of that convenient instrument, an old English Parliament, they stripped him of all his offices and deprived him of his title. Warwick was now all powerful. He captivated the young King by his pretended zeal in promoting the Reformation. He distributed the royal favors with a liberal hand. He instituted the Marquis of Dorset, the father of Jane Grey, the Duke of Suffolk. The Earl of Wiltshire was made a Marquis, as was also Sir William Herbert, and on several others he bestowed the order of Knighthood. Nor did he forget himself. Thomas Percy, Earl of Northumberland, had been decapitated by Henry VIII., and the great title was vacant. He obtained a grant of that vast domain from the King. It had been one of the kingdoms of the ancient Saxon heptarchy. Warwick was now Duke of Northumberland, but he was the only one of his family who bore the name, for the noble house of Percy were restored to their ancient possessions by one of the first acts of Mary when she came to the throne.

The way was now open to the deadly ambition of Warwick. The health of the young King began to decline and it seemed to him that the time was about to arrive when he could follow the giant shadow of the Warwick of old, and like him, make and unmake the Kings of England. He, however, thought it expedient to propose a marriage between Edward and the daughter of France. Although nothing came of it beyond a diplomatic correspondence about the contract, it placed a barrier to all but the formal intercourse of the Court circle between the young King and Jane Grey, for until the engagement should be dissolved they could be nothing to each other except

VI.

schoolfellows, or weaker still, cousins, or perhaps conditions of friendship not sufficient to temper the
clashing interests of life.   The deeper the uncertainty that hung over Edward's health, the darker
grew the anticipations of circles whose future depended
upon his life.   Northumberland was absolute.   He
had immeasurably transcended the despotism of the
last Protector.   If the King died, all experience presaged a repetition of the horrors remembered in the
War of the Roses, which men yet alive had witnessed
to their sorrow and ruin.   Englishmen knew that in
those fierce convulsions a hundred princes of the
blood had perished and fattened the ground; that two
whole generations of the great Warwick, Somerset,
and Percy families were annihilated in the field or on
the scaffold, and their almost royal domains were forfeited or wasted; that the common people had poured
out their tide of life, and that the soil had been deluged
with the blood of its own children; that religion itself,
stripped of every benign or holy attribute, stood an
implacable hireling at the side of carnage, or lighted
the flames of persecution at the stake; and they were
fearful of a return to scenes of such general and bewildering ferocity.   Indeed, there were no indications to
allay their fears, except that to all appearances the

surest bulwark against coming convulsions was presented in the power and sagacity of the new head of
the Government. His religious opinions and conversation were far from intolerant in a time of such
heated polemics that different sects only discussed
each other's principles in such terms as heresy, schism,
idolatry, profanity, blasphemy, wickedness, and voted
all other Christian churches except their own to be
the enemy of God and man and worse than worshipers
of the Devil. The Suffolk family was one of those
most certainly liable to be drawn into the whirlpool
of a civil war. Northumberland felt the pressure of
this perilous fact as fully as they themselves, but was
possessed at the same time with a conviction that
this great interest would of all others be respected in
case the Protestants and Catholics should break out in
open conflagration respecting the claims of Mary and
Elizabeth. He, therefore, effected the union of his
son, Guildford Dudley, with Lady Jane Grey. Neither
side, perhaps, confided its inmost satisfaction to the
other, but both were sanguine that this combination
would extend a reciprocal protection. Had he paused
there, this end had been indubitably gained. Alas!
for the prescience of man; each future step dazzled
both families to a common destruction. The king-

dom now breathlessly awaited the result of the King's
malady.   It terminated we know mortally.   From the
hour he ceased to breathe it seemed as if every step of
Northumberland was a voluntary advance to destruction.   He concealed the demise until he thought Mary
Tudor was allured into his power, and in the meantime, through an inconceivable want of energy and
foresight, permitted an emissary to warn her of the
danger.   He trusted to his own popularity when he
was hated for the death of Somerset.   He relied upon
the support of a nobility who regarded him as a par-
venu and charlatan.   He deputed others to act where
his own authority was indispensable, and appeared in
scenes where his presence turned the tide against him.
But he had been bred a soldier and at least acted with
promptness.   The moment he was satisfied that Mary
was beyond his toils in the great fortress of the heptarchy, Framingham Castle, he hesitated no longer;
and now we come to that phase in the life of Jane
Grey that will interest, perhaps, more than any other.

  She had reached her seventeenth year, and the
young King was dead; but like his father before him,
he left a will in which he devised the crown and royal
estate to his cousin, Jane Grey.   Henry VIII. had
excluded his oldest sister, Margaret, and her descend-

ants, who were represented by Mary Stuart, who was then in France, a child of twelve years. In like manner Edward excluded his sisters and gave the crown to the descendants of his father's youngest sister, who was represented in the person of Jane Grey. The two cases are almost identical. If Edward was the rightful King of England, upon the same facts and principles Jane Grey was equally entitled to the royal estate. It is said, however, that Henry was authorized by an Act of Parliament to leave the crown to whom he pleased, so that after all his will might be regarded as a statutory settlement of the sovereign powers. It was also said that the crown of England could not be diverted from the order of succession, except by the supreme authority of the Parliament. This, however, is a question that did not arise, for the reason that there were statutory inhibitions against the two daughters of Henry VIII. declaring them ineligible on account of illegitimacy, and Edward by failing to recognize them had cogently confirmed the objection. Under these circumstances the council representing the supreme authority of the land was summoned, and proceeded in state to the palace which contained the young person to whose temples the diadem was offered. Until that moment Jane Grey was utterly ignorant of

the King's will.   Her astonishment at the ceremonious
respect with which the grave assemblage asked for an
interview, was only exceeded by incredulous amaze-
ment when they besought her to accept the crown.
As the bewildering announcement fully dawned upon
her perceptions, and all its consequences rushed into
her quick intelligence—her kindred to the dispossessed
fugitive; her intimacy with a princess whose flight
was announced; the friendship that had united them
from her childhood until but yesterday; the letters in
which Mary had blessed her marriage, and the pearls
sent her cousin to keep for her sake; the books they
two had read so often together, sealed, indeed, from so
many of the unenlightened, but luminous to their cultivated minds; and more appalling than all, the dizzy,
floating heights from which she was to survey the
rushing seas of faction and warring successions, or
stretch forth her hand to calm the uprisings of a people
driven mad by the goads of intolerance; and as the
truth took possession of her half-stunned faculties, she
attempted to address the bearers of a crown and
sceptre.   In the effort to speak she fainted away
before them; awakened to consciousness she refused
the perilous gifts.

No declinature was ever more sincerely made, nor,

perhaps, more reasonably entertained. Her tears and
agitation witnessed her attachment to the home now
doubly dear since her marriage. She told them that
her temperament was unsuited to the main features of
the life they proposed; that she was incapable of its
deep cares; that the glare of court magnificence con-
fused without gratifying her senses, and the severities
inseparable from the epoch would destroy her peace of
mind. They listened to her advocacy of the claims of
Mary and Elizabeth as preferable to her own; she
depicted the dark semblance of ingratitude she, above
all others, would incur by supplanting the sisters of
Edward. She averred her love for literature and pursuits which sequestered their followers from the
dangers under which society had trembled ever since
she was born. It was well known by all, she said,
how greatly she disliked and dreaded the trammels of
artificial life, but she alone could be aware of her own
incompetency to fulfill the duties of a Queen over
their unmanageable race. If the crown must pass from
the English princesses, she begged them to send to
Scotland or France for Mary Stuart, who was born a
Queen and was descended from the oldest sister of
Henry.

At last, worn out with sweeping and contending

emotions, she left these noblemen and closited herself in her own apartments.

There is a possibility that after all her determination might have remained final had not a vivid appeal been made to her sense of duty, and her conscience enlisted on the side of accepting the crown.   When her mother entered the room she found her on her knees imploring the aid of Heaven to enlighten her embarrassed path.   It would have been impossible for her to have refused the importunities of her father, who had gone too far to recede, or of her mother, whose fate was identified with her own.   Neither could she be deaf to the entreaties of her husband, whose wish was almost the voice of a command, and who would share every peril that might befall her.   If her opposition had continued immovable, it was in their power to proclaim her the Queen and irrevocably cross the Rubicon without her consent.   But she yielded to all these influences and entreaties timidly, and with trembling reluctance the final step was taken; and no course was left them but to defend it by force of arms.

CHAPTER V.

Lady Jane Grey Occupied the Tower as a Temporary Residence. The People Divided in Opinion. Mary Fortified Framingham Castle. She was Proclaimed Queen in Several Places. Asserted Her Title to the Council. They Advise Her to Submit to Her Lawful Sovereign, Lady Jane Grey. Mary Promised the Protestants to Respect Their Religion. They Espoused the Cause of Mary. Forces Levied for Jane Grey Go Over to Mary. Northumberland Marches Against the Enemy. Sends Back for Reënforcements. The Council Withdraw Their Allegiance from the Reigning Queen. They Proclaim Mary as Queen in London. The Tower Surrendered. Northumberland Himself Proclaims Mary the Queen. Arrested as a Traitor to Both Queens. No Enthusiasm for Either Queen. Northumberland, His Character and Conduct. Mary, Queen of England. Her Visit to the Tower, and the Lady Jane Did Not Object to the Change. Her Fortitude and Resignation. Resumed Her Studies. Her Statement to the Queen. Mary and the Prisoners in the Tower. Funeral of Edward. Death of Northumberland. Lady Jane Furnished the Queen With the Details of Her Royalty. Her Execution Urged for State Reasons. Mary at First Disposed to Mercy. Meeting of Parliament. Catholic Ceremonies Introduced. The Protestants Alarmed. Bill of Attainder Against Jane and Her Husband. Her Serenity Unaffected. Her Treatment in Prison Indulgent. Mary Seemed Inclined to Clemency. Dr. Edwin Sandys.

CHAPTER V.

ACCORDING to the custom of these days, Lady Jane Grey being proclaimed Queen of England, in the City of London, proceeded to occupy the Tower as a temporary residence. The Council accompanied her retinue to the walls that, since William the Norman, had been for five centuries the voiceless confidant of tragedies no human tongue survived to divulge.

The people, divided in opinion, some luke-warm, others timid, and all agitated with the liveliest concern, looked on with an acquiescence that seldom rose into enthusiasm. The Protestant lords had entire control, it is true, of all the authority and forces in the kingdom, and the counsellors declared with the highest protestations their reliance upon Northumberland and the success of their banners under such a leader. The sincerity of their declarations might have been, however, in a measure superficial, for they were, in

fact, prisoners as well as courtiers within the moats
and portcullises of that gloomy hold, the Tower.
This sultry quiet was only the inhalation of the storm
before its breath was unchained; and events followed
with the rapidity of a tempest.

Mary, instead of taking flight from the seaport in
sight of Framingham to pass into Flanders, in order
to address the subject of her wrongs to her powerful
kinsman, the Emperor Charles, who desired her hand
for his son Philip, placed the old castle in a state of
defense and rallied the well-disposed around her standard. In the meantime she had been proclaimed at
Norwich and other towns adjacent to this position.
The Council, to whom she asserted her title to the
throne and offered amnesty and favor, replied not
only by proclaiming Jane Grey, but told her in plain
terms that she had neither a title nor a name under
the law made and provided for dealing with bastard
children; that she was the "*filius nullius*," like her
half-brother, Henry Fitzroy, Duke of Richmond, and
concluded their answer by advising her to submit to
her lawful sovereign Jane, by the Grace of God Queen
of England. They also offered their services to inter-
cede in her behalf. But the peasantry and yeomen of
the County Suffolk remembered the hideous cruelty

with which Northumberland had crushed their religious insurrection during the Protectorate of Somerset;
and after some propitiatory harangues and promises to
respect their religion, the Protestants made common
cause with the Catholics, and espoused that of
Mary.   In ten days after the death of Edward, a fleet
sent by the Council to blow the grey fortress about
the ears of its garrison, mutinied in her favor and furnished enough ordnance and ammunition to arm its
walls from turret to foundation stone.   Sir Edward
Hastings, who had levied 4000 men in the midland
counties to sustain Jane Grey, went over to Mary with
his whole force, and the nucleus of an immense camp
hourly increased around the slopes of her headquarters.
Ere long 10,000 men under arms were reported in
readiness to march against London from another
portion of the interior, and the shipping at Harwick
sent in its adhesion.   In London, Northumberland
had embodied a large force to protect the Tower; but
he dreaded the cabals of his own associates, and felt
that everything depended upon his own presence near
the Queen.   At length danger began to menace him
from every side; the troops of Mary were in battle
array between Framingham and the metropolis—the
lords of the Council induced him to march against

them, as the most fitted by profession and experience
to encounter the enemy. The departure from London
was far from being ominous of good, or from inspiring
ardor into his army. Disaffection had spread to the
populace, who looked upon his marching columns
with such eminent disfavor that he bitterly observed to
Lord Grey, "Many come out to look at us, but I see
none that cry 'God speed you.'" At the famous old
town of Bury St. Edmonds he encountered a force
twice exceeding his own in number; he was unable to
make a serious demonstration, and falling back to
Cambridge instantly sent back fifty miles to London
for reënforcements. The Council, under pretense of
hurrying additional troops into the field, left the Duke
of Suffolk nearly alone in the Tower, and once more
free from confinement, proceeded to deal with the
absent Northumberland as he had taught them to deal
with Somerset. The Earl of Pembroke, Oxford, and
others withdrew their allegiance, Lord Sussex and
Lord Bath gathered their retainers and hastened to
offer their services to Mary at Framingham. The next
day Lord Arundel abandoned Lady Jane Grey, and
others seeing that her cause was hopeless vied with
each other in forsaking the innocent young Queen.
The Marquis of Winchester, Lord Pembroke, and other

of the nobles who had most strenuously solicited her
to accept the crown, gave an early example of defec-
tion, forgetting their pledges and their oaths, and
throwing themselves into the camp of her implacable
foe. The seceding nobles met together, and having
called in the Lord Mayor and City Magistrates, the
Earl of Dundee addressed them, declaring himself most
strongly in favor of their legitimate sovereign, to
whom he was ready to swear allegiance and fidelity.
Then Pembroke, drawing his sword, cried out with
passionate eloquence that if the arguments of the Earl
were not sufficiently persuasive, he would bring to
their aid that of the sword in order to bestow the
crown on Mary. And after exhausting the store
of invectives against Northumberland's treason, as
his conduct was now termed, the conclave, one and
all, rushed into the street and proclaimed Mary as
Queen for the first time in the principal city of
the kingdom. The people expressed their satisfaction by the usual uproar, and a counter-revolution
stood confessed without a blow being struck. Northumberland was hardly an object of interest beyond the
price Mary had set on his head—£1000, if taken and
delivered to the Queen by a nobleman; £500, if so
captured and disposed of by a knight; and £100, if a

yeoman was similarly favored by the chances of war. At Cambridge the Vice-Chancellor of the University preached a sermon against the title and religion of Mary. The news reached his army that the Tower had been beset, and that the Duke of Suffolk, finding resistance useless, had opened the gates and lowered the standard and surrendered it to the insurgents.

One would naturally wonder what a man in such a dilemma would think of doing. His compeers had not only severed the connection in a most unceremonious manner, but were using his name as a scapegoat of all their several iniquities. His army had melted into air from his sight, and reappeared comfortably bivouacked among Mary's battalions. In fact, his cause had melted away also, for when Suffolk surrendered the Tower the drama closed, the lights were blown out, and the actors hid themselves in common apparel. He stood alone as a prodigious conspirator, without any conspiracy to conspire about. Suicide would have seemed the sole alternative to ordinary people. But Northumberland never dreamed of falling upon his own sword. He merely looked for a moment at the capabilities of his situation and then himself proclaimed Mary Queen. He threw his cap into the air and cried, "God save Queen Mary," until the tears ran down his cheeks. He then changed his armor for a court dress in which to pay homage to his liege, when his bosom confidant, Sir John Gates, the most nefarious of all his agents, finding his master with one of his heavy mailed boots half off and the other half on, seized him by the collar and arrested him in Her Majesty's name. He surrendered himself quietly, but as soon as he got both boots off his feet, he knocked Sir John down with one of them, and arrested him as a traitor to both Queens. As he had only one head, Mary took the first choice and brought it to the block in five days afterwards.

The arrival of Arundel at the head of the Queen's guards ended the farce, by placing a platoon over both the Duke and the knight and sending them to London.

The only comfort left was the hope, common to all on the losing side, "that Queen Mary was a merciful woman, and doubtless all would receive the benefit of a general pardon." It would be remarkable that the proclamation of Jane in London and Mary in Norwich excited no cries of applause; that the appeals and exhortations of both factions seemed to fall upon a people in the last stage of supineness, or rather of lethargic indifference, had we not an accurate knowledge of the meagre appliances at command of either

VII.

side. When Mary gained intelligence of the pitfall which had decoyed her to London the day after Edward's death, she was in an open plain, on horseback, without any escort save the steward of her household, the ladies who resided with her, and a few grooms and horse boys to guard her luggage. She had neither money, soldiers, nor advisers. She was even unable to form a plan, much less to execute one, and still inaction was the most perilous of all. This information might, after all, be false, and Edward still alive. If she proclaimed herself Queen it would be an act of open and aggressive treason, perhaps the very fruit of a snare laid by the Council, who intended that she should compromise herself by a royal proclamation. On the other hand, if she held on her course to London, and found Edward no more, their other object would be gained, for the Tower was awaiting her. On the spur of the moment she resolved upon two very sensible plans—to canter as fast as their jennets would carry them toward the coast, and keep the secret of her misgivings to herself until they reached a friendly neighborhood. The people along the road were told the plague had broken out at her country seat, Hounsdon, and that they were hurrying for a change of air to another mansion at

Kenninghall. The only roof under which they slept during the flight was never to shelter a human tenant again. As the cavalcade gained the summit of the Gozonagay hills they saw their hospitable shelter in flames and pillaged by a mob. Had they been less intent upon plunder she would have suffered an easy capture ; well that her morning mass was short and her journey sped before the sun rose upon it. The present superb structure of Swanson Hall was rebuilt at her expense and presented to her protector in that perilous emergency.

It is a striking evidence of the wild and unpeopled state in that day of those counties, now so fertile and populous, that the change of route and eccentric detours of Mary's party drew upon it no greater attention through the tract they passed over, and that their escape from so important an edifice at daylight did not arouse the country in advance of their direction.

Says one of our most respectable authorities, "Not so much for the love of Mary, but from hatred to the Duke of Northumberland, the accession of Jane Grey fell coldly upon the people." He had an immunity from scruples of every kind that allowed any piece of abstract wickedness to become a part of his measures; but he put them into execution without energy or address. As he called in question nothing that could serve his turn, so nothing was easier than to have requested Edward to write for both his sisters and to have made sure of their persons before he struck the final blow. Neither was there much difficulty in procuring the absence of Mary in the low countries, where the power of the Emperor then extended. Had Northumberland seen that he was well served, as all men must when engaged in doing such hazardous attempts, he could have got possession of the ancient battlements of Framingham long before Hastings deserted him with the levies made in Lady Jane's name. When he discovered that his popularity was altogether illusory, he had the means to act with the strong hand and coerce where he could not persuade. He squandered his time in playing the prompter behind the scenes, and only awoke to action when the face of external society had changed and set as flint against him.

The transformation of affairs was so rapid that on the 22d of the same month Mary dismissed her militia, and set out for the seat of government, and in a few days entered it as the undisputed Queen of England.

When the gates of the Tower were thrown open, the insignia of royalty passed from the fair being

these winged hours had borne to the summit of
human splendor, and as suddenly cast down; but the
Lady Jane did not object to the change, for it restored
the happy lot she had changed for the throne. She
ordered the distinctive marks of state to be taken
away, and the ceremonial in her presence to be ended.
To those who were willing to sustain her, so young
and overtaken by so great a vicissitude, she set the
example of fortitude and resignation. "This is a
more welcome summons," she said, "than that which
forced me against my will to an elevation to which I
am not entitled, and for which I am not qualified.
For obedience to you, my lord," addressing her father,
"and to my mother, I did violence to myself; the
present is my own act and I willingly resign." Her
life was now happier than before she had been a
Queen. The pageantry and meaningless form of
courts had been revealed to her; the waste of time
and heartless intercourse which the conventional insin-
cerity of a palace sanctioned, induced her regret and
disapproval; the pompous indirection affairs of the
least importance put in requisition revolted while it
amused her clear and direct sense; the general aspect
of guile which could be seen peeping out of the fairest
exterior mortified her ingenuous, upright nature, and

the remorseless sacrifice of friendship, natural affection, and personal honor in pursuit of baubles opened the recesses where human corruptions lurked. The period passed as a Queen she regarded as so much time lost from her usual avocations. On her retirement from the throne she took them up precisely where they had been laid down, and continued her studies and order of reading as if they had been interrupted by illness or an ususual number of visitors.

We can easily believe her own statement to Queen Mary regarding her reluctance to leave the real pleasures of her life. She says in discussing the transaction: "As soon as I had, with infinite pain to my mind, understood these things, how much I was beside myself, stunned and agitated, I leave to these lords to testify who saw me fall to the ground and who know how grievously I wept."

We have every reason to think that Mary, overjoyed at her good fortunes, felt a generous impulse toward her enemies, and cherished merciful purposes toward them. As nothing breathes a more desolate sentiment than the separation and farewell of those mutually dear, so few incidents of life are more affecting than their restoration through peril and terror to each other. Of this nature was the meeting of Mary with the state prisoners in the Tower. Kneeling before the Queen in front of St. Peter's Church were the old Duke of Suffolk, the greatest temporal prince of her realm, saved from execution by the death of Henry before his death warrant was signed, and the Earl of Devonshire, her cousin, grown up in prison, from his tenth to his thirtieth year. He had already forgotten how to sign his name. Among the many suppliants were also the deprived Bishops, among whom the greatest of them, Gardiner, addressed the new sovereign and implored her clemency on behalf of them all.

Mary burst into tears as she recognized the features of those unjustly detained by her father and brother, and extending her hands to them exclaimed, "Ye are now my prisoners." She raised them one by one, kissing their foreheads, and ordered their instant liberation. The haughty Duchess of Somerset, a prisoner since the execution of her husband, was re-instated in her rank and fortune; her three daughters, who, during her degradation, had been placed with their relatives, re-assembled under their mother's roof to hope for the future, if they could not forget the past.

A month had elapsed from the death of Edward; a magnificent funeral now awaited his remains; the only obstacle was of a religious nature. Those entering into wedlock are occasionally united, even in our day, by the Catholic as well as the Protestant forms of marriage, an interval occurring between the double rite; but the obsequies of Edward present a solitary instance of being performed simultaneously according to the rituals of both religions. As the late King was buried with the Church of England service, by the Archbishop of Canterbury, Mary absented herself from a ceremony she esteemed heretical; but caused a mass appropriate to the occasion to be celebrated in her private chapel; she assisted with the ladies of her court in a solemn dirge and requiem for the repose of the dead. He had at least the evidence of respect from both sides of the religious question to recommend his character in the other world.

The enormous guilt of Northumberland forbade the most sanguine to hope for his pardon. Yet Holinshed, upon whom we rely for so many facts, assures us that Mary was with great difficulty induced to sign his death warrant. But the truth appears to be that public executions had become an adjunct of a new accession.

The order of the Dahomey pageant was reversed, and instead of rivers of blood to commemorate the end

of a reign, our ancestors required a propitiatory liba-
tion before their monarchs were crowned, and felt
aggrieved with the parsimony of Mary's vengeance.
She only indulged them with the death of Northumberland and two of his followers before her coronation.
The people, however, made the most of the spectacle
by flaunting before the Duke's eyes the handkerchiefs
they had dipped in the blood of Somerset.

At the desire of the Queen the Lady Jane furnished
her with a narrative of her brief royalty, beginning its
details at the moment the death and testamentary dis-
positions of the King were announced to her.   We
owe the preservation of these ingenuous and pity-
moving effusions to the industry of Italian historians,
this interval of her life being lost in English archives,
and probably contained in the correspondence of the
Italian Ambassador.   It is only necessary to repeat
the substance of these relations.   She graphically
describes her wonder and consternation when for the
first time in her life her own mother approached her
with the homage due only to a sovereign; when the
Duke, her father, and lords who were the counsellors
and executors of Edward's will read it to her upon
their knees; when her husband cast down his eyes as
if before a stranger; and when she was told that her

duty to God and the realm enjoined an absolute and
lawful obedience to their summons.   She narrates how,
from the first, a conviction weighed down upon her
that she was only the passive victim of an ambition
which consulted neither her inclination, happiness, nor
safety.   That she lost her consciousness and swooned
from the certainty of being helpless in such unrelenting hands, as much as from a presentiment of coming
catastrophes.   These avowals also lay bare the familiar particulars of consultations over the robes she
should wear, the apartments to be occupied, and the
estate to which her husband was to be elevated.
These deliberations were naturally frequent and prolix,
as no Queen Regnant had yet succeeded to the crown.
Indeed, she accords that if anything can extenuate her
fault in yielding to persuasion against the voice of her
conscience and principles, it can only be found in a
truthful and ingenuous disclosure.   Her emotions are
vividly expressed when the crown of state was
brought to her.   She felt a superstitious horror when
requested to place it upon her head.

The Dudleys had determined that her husband
should be crowned as well as herself, and she drew
upon herself "violent treatment," which we must
presume was confined to words alone, when she

firmly set herself against an arrogation so intolerable.

These were many of the facts of which she unbosomed herself to her Queen and relative, and far from being insensible to the incontestable truth of these acknowledgments, her royal cousin sat mercifully in judgment upon her—and with the more merit to herself it may be fairly argued, for the imperial Ambassadors urged the equity of Jane's execution under the plea so fruitful of crime and cruelty—state necessity; no security, they maintained, could exist for the Queen's life so long as another crowned head in the kingdom was left unlopped, for every faction that rose would declare it the object of their allegiance. There had been in former times some vicious talk carried to Mary's ears; it was now renewed with enormous industry. The reporter was a friend of the Lady Jane; the subject, herself. It was nothing more reprehensible than a perfectly just, but cutting, *bon-mot*, directed in chance conversation at an occurrence in the Queen's chapel; but joined in an officious and malignant spirit to other conversations, a less friendly regard was infused into Mary's mind, that never forgot a bad point in anybody. She resented, however, the advice of the Spanish envoys; she went further, and became Jane's advocate. She placed her in the light

of an innocent, mistaken instrument of the usurpation.
Nor did she hesitate to say that her cousin was the
only one in the two families who was not Northumberland's accomplice; that she herself knew how to
estimate the risk of a pardon better than the ambassadors, for she was the born child of danger and its companion for more than thirty years; moreover, she
spurned the cowardly justification they harped upon,
and instead of sacrificing so much innocence and goodness, she intended to take every precaution to free this
lovely young person from the Dudley connection
before she was set at liberty. By this she would
be enabled to make her what nature and education
had intended, the greatest ornament of the English
court; for apart from her family the Lady Jane had no
pretensions or aspirations of her own, but was loyalty
itself. A confidence was, therefore, encouraged by
this evidence of Mary's clement intentions that if she
were brought to trial it would be for the simple purpose of being discrowned with a solemnity equal to
that of her coronation. For this purpose an opportunity was soon to be afforded by the opening of Parliament. Three months had nearly elapsed since the
deposition of Jane Grey, when this body came together
under omens that terrified the Protestants of England

and of all Christendom. It commenced the session by celebrating before both houses the mass of the Holy Ghost in Latin, with all the rites and ceremonies abolished by law. The Bishops of Lincoln and Hertford, who refused to kneel, were violently thrust out of the Abbey with no little scandal and confusion. A chaplain who approached with a censor to cense the Queen was collared by Dr. Weston, saying, "She won't be censed by a married priest; go and cense your moppet."*

After repealing and amending many of the infernal statutes of Henry VIII., the legitimacy of Mary was established by law. A bill of attainder was found against both Jane and Guildford Dudley, these being the only titles accorded to them. They both pleaded guilty; she was sentenced to be beheaded on Tower Hill, or burnt alive, according to the Queen's will. The crowds that had been so inert at the crisis of her fate, when Mary was proclaimed, at once appeared to be touched with the most active sympathy for her accumulated misfortunes. Thousands followed her back to the Tower, bewailing her doom and endeavoring to catch a word from her lips or a glimpse of her features. Her deportment was unaffected, dignified,

*This occurred at the funeral of Edward, not at the Parliament.

and serious, and as we have high authority for repeating the expression, "angelic in its meekness"; she consoled her husband with thoughts that rose above the world, and proved how triumphantly a life of piety, philosophy, and good deeds had prepared her for this dreadful moment. Jane Grey believed in immortality. It was her ideal. It is this faith which marks great souls. There are many mournful circumstances associated with death, in order that man may not yield himself up to self-destruction and attempt too soon to rush into the future life. Immortality is the universal instinct of mankind. It is the recompense for the ills of life, for duty well performed, for sacrifice, for martyrdom. Its desire is inextinguishable. It elevates us towards all those whom we have lost and restores us to them again. It purifies us and moralizes the entire nature. It is the spiritual end towards which it is sweet and noble to gravitate with confidence. In believing in immortality we err not, we are on our path, we walk, we fly to our divine home, where our ancestors await us. It is the star of our night, the Pharos of the tempests, the harbor of our journey.

Intimations from the court soon acquired currency that it was not intended to exact this last penalty of her sentence. The unusual indulgences immediately extended were taken as the forerunners of a full pardon. Nothing incompatible with safe detention was withheld from her. She received her friends, continued her correspondence, and had access to books and the current topics of the day. And finally, though not until the very last, the Queen's garden was open to her for exercise within its walls, and no objection was made to her extending her walk upon Tower Hill. There can be no doubt that Mary from policy—it is easy to say, but more just and charitable to believe from merciful considerations—had resolved upon her cousin's restoration to herself and to the world. Other acts pointed to a placable temper in the Queen. No one had been more bitter and trenchant in denouncing her title, religion, and pretensions than Dr. Edwin Sandys, Vice-Chancellor of Cambridge, the same who preached a violent sermon against her at the request of Northumberland, the day previous to his submission. But these attacks and insults had not closed her heart to intercession in his favor. It is told that one day the Bishop of Winchester came to the Privy Council, when the following dialogue took place between him and the Queen:

"What do you think of Dr. Sandys?" said Her Majesty. It must be understood that the persons who appealed to Mary procured her promise that if Gardiner placed no difficulties in the way she was willing that the prosecution of Sandys should be withdrawn. The same intercession had wrought upon the Bishop to agree with the Queen if she discovered a favorable disposition to the prisoner.

"As it pleases Your Majesty," he answered, awaiting his cue from her humor.

"Well," said the Queen, "to speak truly, we would have the saucy Churchman set at liberty."

Although somewhat out of the order of events I desire to give a copy of a letter which Roger Ascham wrote to Jane in the early part of the year 1551, while he was on some kind of a mission on the Continent. It is as follows:

"In this my long peregrination, most illustrious lady, I have travelled far; have visited the greatest cities; and have made the most diligent observations in my power upon the manners of nations, their institutions, laws, religion, and regulations; nevertheless, in such variety there is nothing that has raised in me greater admiration than what I found in regard to yourself during the last summer, to see one so young and lovely, even in the absence of her learned preceptor, in the noble hall of her family, at the very moment when all her friends and relatives were enjoying hunting and field sports—to find, I repeat, oh, all ye gods! so divine a maid diligently perusing the divine Phaedon of Plato; in this more happy, it may be believed, than in her noble and royal lineage.

"Go on thus, oh best adored virgin, to the honor of thy country, the delight of thy parents, thy own glory, the praise of thy preceptor, the comfort of thy relatives and acquaintances, and the admiration of all. Oh happy Elmer! to have such a scholar, and to be her preceptor. I congratulate both you who teach, and she who learns.

"These are the words of John Sturmius unto myself as my reward for teaching the most illustrious Lady Elizabeth; but to you two I can repeat them even with more truth; to you two I concede this felicity, even though I should have to lament want of success where I had expected to reap the sweetest fruits from my labor.

"'But let me restrain the sharpness of my grief, which prudence makes it necessary I should conceal even to myself. This much I may say, that I have no fault to find with the Lady Elizabeth, whom I have always found the best of ladies, nor indeed with the Lady Mary; but if ever I shall have the happiness to meet my friend Elmer, then shall I repose in his bosom my sorrows abundantly.'

"Two things I repeat to thee, my good Elmer—for I know that thou wilt see this letter—that by your persuasion and entreaty the Lady Jane Grey, as early as she can conveniently, may write to me in Greek, which she has already promised to do. I have even written lately to John Sturmius, mentioning this promise. Pray let your letter and hers fly together to us. The distance is great, but John Hales will take care that it shall reach me. If she even were to write to Sturmius himself in Greek, neither you nor she shall have cause to repent your labor.

"The other request is, my good Elmer, that you would exert yourself so that we might conjointly preserve this mode of life amongst us. How freely, how sweetly, and philosophically, then, should we live! Why should we, my good Elmer, less enjoy all these good things, which Cicero, at the conclusion of his third

VIII.

book, De Finitus, describes as the only rational mode of life? Nothing in any tongue, nothing in any times, in human memory, either past or present, from which something may not be drawn to sweeten life.

"As to the news here, most illustrious lady, I know not what to write. That which is written of stupid things, must itself be stupid; and, as Cicero complained of his own times, there is little to amuse, or that can be embellished. Besides, at present all places and persons are occupied with rumors of wars and commotions, which for the most part are either mere fabrications, or founded upon no authority; so that anything respecting continental politics would neither be interesting nor useful to you.

"The general council of Trent is to sit on the first of May: Cardinal Pole, it is asserted, is to be the president. Besides, there are tumults this year in Africa; then preparations for a war against the Turks; and then the great expectations of the march of the Emperor into Hungary, of which, though no soldier, I shall, God willing, be a companion. Why need I write to you of the siege of Medgeburg, and how the Duke of Mechlenburg has been taken; or of that commotion which so universally at this moment afflicts the miserable Saxony? To write of all these things I have neither leisure nor would it be safe; but on my return, which I hope is not far distant, it shall be my great happiness to relate all these things to you in person.

"Thy kindness to me, oh most noble Jane Grey, was always most grateful to me when present with you; but it is ten times more so during this long absence. To your noble parents I wish length of happiness; to you a daily victory in letters and in virtue; to thy sister Katharine, that she may resemble thee; and to Elmer I wish every good that he may wish to Ascham.

"Further, dearest lady, if I were not afraid to load thee with the weight of my light salutations, I would ask thee, in my name to salute Elizabeth Astley, who, as well as her brother John, I believe to be of my best friends; and whom I believe to be like that brother in all integrity and sweetness of manners.

"Salute, I pray thee, my cousin Mary Laten, and my wife Alice, of whom I think oftener than I can now express. Salute, also, that worthy young man Garret and John Haddon.

"Farewell, most noble lady in Christ.

"R. A.

"AUGUSTAE, 18th January, 1551."

It would be a singular sight, even in this enlightened age—that of a girl of fourteen years corresponding with the first scholars of Europe, and in Greek—Ascham, Bullinger, and Sturmius. Her own letters to Bullinger are in Latin and unaffected in feeling, pure in style, and the sentiments religious. The story of her virtues and accomplishments is incontrovertible. She forgot that nature had endowed her with all that could adorn so great a station, and preferred the claim of her rival to enjoy it. If her possession of power infringed the rights of others, it was in its manner the most innocent usurpation the world ever witnessed. It bore higher moral grandeur than the abdication of Charles V. intrinsically sustained. He surrendered an imperial badge which had ceased to exalt or gratify. She accepted a sovereignty she both dreaded and disliked. His son, at the paternal command, ascended a throne thus left vacant to govern empires spread on both hemispheres. Jane Grey exchanged patrician life for royal state under the adjuration of a dying predecessor, and yielded it without regret and fled back to the peaceful retirement from which she had been forced. Little can be wondered that a deed so nefarious as her execution, without cause and profitless, stamped the Queen of England as a monster throughout Christendom, and caused her subjects in foreign lands to conceal a birthplace so soaked in blood.

CHAPTER VI.

CHAPTER VI.

HE Queen's marriage became a matter of anxiety and forethought, not only to the statesmen of that day, but to all the people of England. Her fancy was thought to have been captivated by the young Courtnay, Earl of Devon, whom she found in the Tower. In reality no pains were spared on her part to supply by education the deficiencies under which he labored. Among other good offices a tutor of rank was selected to train him into conformity with his fine intellect, handsome person, and, if possible, to discard the habits of swearing, drinking, and gambling, which he had brought into society from the Tower. This match would have been most pleasing to her subjects, who pitied his romantic misfortunes and admired his good looks. But after much vacillation the choice of her Council fell at last upon Philip of Spain.

The whole nation became alarmed, not that the

main objection hinged upon the alliance being a foreign one. No objection existed on the score of age or opulence, for Spain had seized the mines of Mexico, and bullion was so abundant with its heir that he brought to London a hundred chests, each a yard and a quarter long, filled with coin and precious metals. The Prince was also ten years younger than the Queen. The popular antipathy to the match was founded upon reasons sufficiently distinct to engender the wildest accusations. The articles of the marriage contract, which guarded the rights of the Queen, were unsatisfactory to the nation. It was believed that Spain aimed at universal dominion, and in consummating this insidious marriage, contemplated the reduction of England to a province of that empire. They pointed out, fearless of contradiction, that the Netherlands, Milan, Sicily, and Naples were crushed by Spanish tyranny; that the historical atrocities of Attila and Genghis Khan were the transactions of a humane warfare compared to the hideous and unrelenting scenes of Spanish conquest in the New World; that the statutes of Torquemada would supplant the Charter of King John, and the Inquisition, begotten of Iberian cruelty, would send every Protestant to the stake, or into infamy, confiscation, and perpetual captivity. The letter was cited in which the celebrated Vives, writing to Erasmus, deplores the conduct of even moderate and charitable Catholics in Valladolid. He says, "We live in dreadful times; we can neither speak nor be silent without danger." To the Spaniards was also imputed the intention to break open the tombs of the old English Kings, and burn their bones for the heresy of the dead. It was reported that Mary had privately caused the remains of Henry VIII. to be consumed by fire, for his disobedience to the Church of Rome.

By this means opinions, sentiments, and fears were stirred to their depths, and the habits and prejudices of the masses were threatened and alarmed by this marriage, until all classes were wrought to such a pitch that a well-known, vigorous leader, such as Cromwell, Knox, or Montrose, could have torn the Tudor dynasty from its foundations.

The more reflecting portion of the highest classes participated in the universal concernment, but they had wider grounds of disquiet; they feared the hostility of France as much as friendship with Spain. Both were superlative evils, but the mass of active malcontents resolved that it would be easier to prevent the impending mischief than to repair it afterwards. In former reigns there had been the most violent commotions. The English people had learned to manage their kings by extraordinary means and appliances, for they usually rose in arms to prevent the royal encroachments. The monarchs were not disposed to pay the respect that Queen Victoria would to the ceremonies, the checks, the morals, and parliaments of her people. It is not, in fact, apparent how a ruler who forced loans and levied benevolences, who repudiated his foreign wives and truncated his native born ones, could be kept in order by any ordinary means. These were the only restraints upon an inordinate despotism, and they were undoubtedly stronger than any artificial barrier thrown up by law could have been in that rude period. It was the grand and effectual limitation upon kingly encroachments. In previous reigns it had frequently manifested its power: the fate, for instance, of the great Duke of York, who failed to obtain the royal authority he grasped at, and whose head the fierce Margaret of Anjou crowned with a paper diadem and spiked on the gates of his own capital; the fate of Richard II., who, when dethroned and imprisoned in Pontefract Castle, was dispatched by means of starvation; the fate of Edward II., who after a short reign was hurled from his throne and murdered at Berkley Castle, with torments the pen refuses to recount; or of Henry VI., cruelly put to death while a prisoner in the Tower, or of the two young princes immolated in the same gloomy fortress. The Tudor monarchs knew that if the strength of the nation was once put forth it would be found irresistible. Thus Henry VIII., the most cruel of rulers since the days of Domitian, knew that if a large body of his subjects became thoroughly discontented, instead of holding meetings, making royal addresses, and forming associations and combinations, they would rise up; that they would give a Scarborough warning—a word and a blow, but the blow first and the word an evil one—with their bows and helmets, their hauberks and morions, and that he had no means of protecting himself against the public hatred. The Tudors had also discovered there were always men who were unfitted to pursue a regular preferment in the arts, in commerce, or in aspirations to court favor; men who could lead an insurrection or sail a buccaneering cruise upon the Spanish main with equal profit and want of scruple; men at once dexterous marauders and hungry cut-purses, who were always a dangerous element when the sturdy yeomen, who had little but their courage and sturdy frames, stood in need of a leader.

Hence, all the Tudors except Mary courted public favor. The nation granted them the state and respect of something like absolute power—the power to dispose of the lives of their ministers and courtiers, as many bishops as they could catch, and occasionally a cardinal; these people the sovereign had raised up; they were held to be his creatures and natural perquisites; he might abase them as low as he desired, to the bottom of the grave for aught the people cared. But the condition on which they were suffered to be tyrants over their wives, their favorites, and their concubines, was that they should be mild and paternal sovereigns of England.

They even found it dangerous to grind their subjects with cruel taxation. When Henry VIII., says his minister, Sir Thomas More, attempted to raise a force loan by proceedings of unusual rigor, the people assumed such an attitude of determined resistance that his daring will and heart of flint were appalled by their opposition. The nation said, "If we are to be taxed thus, then were it worse than the taxes of France, and England would be bond and not free." Similarly in the time of Elizabeth the monopolies which were granted by her to some statesman or favorite became the subject of general indignation and remonstrance. Yet this courageous Queen, who is represented to us by Hume and other historians as being absolute in the sense of an autocrat, was terrified by the mutterings of the coming storm, and wisely and prudently yielded the point before the colliding clouds of public opinion should in that electric atmosphere emit the thunder and lightning of rebellion. In truth, the government of the Tudors was with a few occasional deviations a free government, with certain royal but disputed prerogatives that taken all together resembled a despotism. It may be said that the prerogatives of Elizabeth were as ample as those of France, that her warrant was equal to a French king's *lettre-de-cachet*. But the power of Louis XIV., for instance, was based on the support of his army. Had this immense mercenary force been uncertain, been corrupted, or had it in any manner failed him, the scene that witnessed the decapitation of Louis XVI., of the French Revolution, of Robespierre, of Marat, of the guillotine, of the fusillades, and, in fine, of the Reign of Terror with all its appurtenances of horrors, would have been anticipated by a century at least.

The Tudors, like the rest of their predecessors, committed some very tyrannical acts, but their power consisted in the willing obedience of their subjects and perhaps in the respect and attachment the common people bore to the race to which they belonged. But Mary, forgetting the popular spirit of concession which had insured the peaceful reigns of her family, paid no respect to the wishes of the people. She was bent on the Spanish match, and the storm which had been threatened broke into war and bloodshed.

Kent, above all other counties the hereditary cradle of insurrections, first took the field. The leader of the Devon insurgents was Sir Thomas Wyatt, and he brought over the Duke of Suffolk by promising to restore the Lady Jane to the throne. The Duke fled from London to raise the dethroned Queen's standard near the old battle-field of Bosworth. The people flocked to Wyatt's banner, and it is observable that his proclamation avoided the subject of religion, and was grounded upon a national hatred to the Spanish race and an aversion to those who counseled a royal union with it. The impatience of the Devonshire people burst forth before a proper agreement with other parts of the Island was effected, their leaders were captured, and the yeomanry took refuge in the vicinity of their homes. Still Wyatt advanced. The old Duke of Norfolk, a mighty champion in his day, led a large force into the South and drew up before the enemy.

To his consternation and mortification the royal troops went over in large numbers, exclaiming that they would not help to make Englishmen Spanish slaves. The London bands, who formed the rear-guard, retreated at the first shot. The cry, "We are all Englishmen!" ran from rank to rank. The Duke ordered them to be shot down with artillery, but the fraternization had become complete, and he escaped with a single aide-de-camp to report the tidings to his mistress. Simultaneously a tremendous disaffection spread all over the city. The ambassadors of foreign powers fled from the metropolis, and were nearly brought into contact with the insurgents, now 15,000 strong.

Indeed, the insurrection had become so formidable that the court opened an ineffectual negotiation with Wyatt. He demanded that the Tower should be placed in his keeping, that four Councillors should be delivered as hostages, and that the Queen should break off the Spanish alliance forever by immediately marrying an Englishman. The terms of pacification contained in this ultimatum were not likely to be listened to by a Queen of the Tudor blood. Unfortunately for the desperate young adventurer (he was not yet twenty-five), the Tower guns bore upon the quarter of

the city which the insurgents occupied. The passage
of London Bridge, then the only one in the neighborhood, was disputed so resolutely that to carry it by
force was out of the question; and the great object of
the royalists was to prevent the junction of the enemy
with their partisans in the city. The Queen had
thrown herself on horseback, and addressed the citizens with spirit and eloquence, and they had answered
with cheers and shouting, "Long live the Queen."
She even ordered her barge and trusted herself within
bow range of the combatants who struggled for the
possession of London Bridge. The possession of Lud-
gate, which was to have been thrown open by his
sympathizers, was irrevocably lost by his detention on
the Surrey bank. By marching up the Surrey border
a few miles Wyatt crossed into Middlesex with four
thousand picked men, and descended upon the palaces
of Whitehall and St. James. The men of Kent, now
separated by a wide river from all aid but their own
valor, addressed themselves to the feat of capturing
the fortified circle that belted in the wealth, the power,
and the discontent of London City. At two o'clock
in the morning a breathless messenger brought intelligence that in an hour the rebels would be in the
parks and gardens of the Queen's palace. The Bishop

of Winchester entreated her to enter a boat and take refuge in the Tower. This she refused to do, and at daybreak, in the midst of a furious rain, two divisions of the invaders rushed through the storm with shouts and deafening yells, one for St. James and the other for Whitehall.

The Queen saw from the window her stalwart guards disposed of and hacked to pieces and driven in upon the palace walls. Fugitives rushed by vociferating that all was lost. The ladies around her shrieked, swooned, and were hopelessly demented by the bloodshed and clangor. But the Queen was undaunted and retained perfect self-possession.

All the well-known streets, the Strand, Pall Mall, and Piccadilly, were then an open space with lanes, villas, and park enclosures; the whole was called St. James's fields, and furnished the arena of the present contest. The plain rang with the shock of battle and the air was tremulous with war cries and reverberating artillery. In front of the palace the death struggle hung long before its gates, but the focus of the combat was now centred at Charing Cross, and was animated with new fury by the presence of Wyatt, who with prodigious effort had reached the heart of the mêlée; a detachment under Kennet, the most dauntless of his

IX.

companions, kept up the onslaught on Whitehall, until
it became almost impossible to distinguish friend from
foe.   Fugitive after fugitive rushed past the palace
hurriedly shouting, "Away, away, a barge, a barge for
the Queen! all is lost, save the Queen!"   Winchester
again sprang into the Queen's presence, crying, "The
battle is broken, all is lost, flight is the only hope!"

The terror in the palace rose to an appalling height
when Mary announced her intention to enter into the
battle and die with the defenders of her crown.
Throwing a heavy cloak around her person she left
the palace, and standing between two harquebusiers
encouraged them to fire, and then awaited the issue in
open air and line of battle.

At length the final charge was made by Pembroke.
Numbers prevailed against the headlong desperation
of the insurgents; they became separated into groups
and were forced down different streets.   Wyatt himself, cut off from his followers, fought for a retreat
with renewed ferocity slowly down Fleet street; at
length, dripping with blood, exhausted and dispirited,
he staggered from the middle of the street and rested
for breath against a stall opposite the Bell Savage
Tower, which was barricaded.   Sir Maurice Berkley,
struck with admiration of his youth, determination,

and personal prowess, approached him unarmed and persuaded him to surrender. He took the exhausted chief on his horse and placed him in the Tower. A contemporary annalist of Kent says regretfully, "He was the godliest fighting man of his years in all Englonde, but to take London is a parlous empress."

The good angel of Mary Tudor had again spread its sheltering wings over her fortunes. By vigilant precautions, judicious treatment of the public excitement, this formidable conspiracy subsided into the nine days' wonder of the town. The truculent citizens and turbulent rabble were overawed by the defeat of their provincial combatants. Discontent was not allayed, but their passions had found escape, and were calmed by the great tragedy they had witnessed. Had the leaders of Wyatt's rebellion pushed their fortunes whilst the first ferment was active in the capital, or had cut short the conferences at Deptford and Southwark, or had they even waited until the revolt had acquired a coherent form in the other martial districts, there was no insuperable obstacle to the seizure of London. The desultory uprisings were put down before they acquired an organization; the handful of men he led up to the city wall should have been strong enough to force their way through it and

appeal to the body of his well-wishers within. After
the dispersal of Norfolk's army all depended upon
celerity of movement, a junction with the guilds, who
were all accustomed to the use of weapons, and
excelled in street encounters. Had he been seconded
by associates of his own daring and intrepidity, the
star that lit Mary's way in the first revolution of her
reign might perhaps have been plunged in darkness
by a second uprising of the people she had estranged.

It may be conjectured without much hazard that
Queen Mary's natural acerbity of temper was not
softened by this last attack upon her power; the
revolted provinces had even besieged her palace and
aimed at laying hands upon her person. The insurrection was put down, and Sir Thomas Wyatt was
beheaded. Four hundred heads were displayed upon
the pinnacles of the bridges, and five hundred insurgents, with ropes around their necks, were led into
the presence of the Queen, who pardoned them. The
Tower was filled with the revolters and gentry suspected of aiding or even of favoring the late insurrection; when it could hold no more the public prisons
received those who were arrested. For Suffolk there
could be little grace; so confident was the Queen of
his loyalty that a commission was engrossed for him to

succeed Norfolk in the command of her forces. The messenger had just ceased to search for him in London, when lo! he was discovered at Rochester in the van of the rebellion. The complication was beyond the cure of royal mercy. His daughter had experienced Mary's clemency for more than six months. He abandoned her while her life hung upon a thread; he seemed determined that it should be snapped by his own temerity. He had been pardoned without even an arraignment, and rebelled again without Northumberland's example for an excuse. This, too, was the special crime for which he had been once forgiven. The Queen had been cajoled into a belief of his sincerity, and whilst relying upon his support of her title and influence among the London populace, he was busy proclaiming her prisoner's right to the crown and practicing treason to herself. Instead of leading her armies, he was in flagrant insurgency against her person and power. In fact, there was little sympathy felt for him in any quarter. Not only had Suffolk abused her confidence, but the rebellion brought to sight thousands who had used their interest and popularity to effect her dethronement or humiliation. The Princess Elizabeth herself could not clear up the suspicious complicity discovered with Wyatt's treason. Courtnay, the Queen's favorite, whom she had loved, watched over, and wished to marry, was undoubtedly a conspirator in league with her younger sister, and perhaps combined to acquire her kingdom for themselves.

The adventures of Elizabeth's early life are romantic, perilous, and in some regards touched with melancholy interest. Her adhesion to Protestantism through the terrors of her sister's reign, though she spoke not of it, vouch for her masculine resolution. The numerous stories of her address and presence of mind have, of course, been put into the shape most decorative for a historical page, but the naked facts of her incredible preservation and magnificent career have placed her forever among the most interesting and illustrious rulers in history. We must remember what the watchful mind of Elizabeth fully penetrated that her sister "panted for her blood."

There are many ways of explaining the unfriendly feeling of her sister. Their close relationship made Elizabeth a rival for the throne itself, and the great body of the reformers regarded her as their only hope, and as the only one upon whom they could concentrate their efforts. The public mind was agitated with the most fearful apprehensions. The stake and the scaffold were doing their terrible work, the pinnacles of London Bridge were surmounted with ghastly heads and limbs, and scores and hundreds of the best in the land had been put to death. Every evidence is corroborative that her secret assassination, if not public extermination, was meditated. The instructions to the troop of horse which arrested her at her home in Hatfield and conveyed her to the Tower in London, were to bring her "quick or dead." They so fully comprehended the spirit of their mission that they exercised the letter of their orders by breaking at dead of night into the apartments where she lay prostrated with illness, and hurried her off at the eminent peril of her life, giving scarcely an opportunity to arrange her garments. The French Ambassador wrote to his court: "The city is covered with gibbets, and the public buildings are crowded with the bravest men in the kingdom. The Princess Elizabeth, for whom no better fate is foreseen, is lying seven or eight miles hence, so swollen and disfigured that it is doubtful she can reach London alive. It can make little difference to her, however, for her death is resolved upon." In the Tower her treatment was unnecessarily harsh. The constable of the fortress, Sir John Gage, was very severe. He had his special orders for this prisoner.

Her servants and women were removed and those of
the Queen were substituted to watch her movements
and her words, and they continually tormented her by
detailing the circumstances of the death of Jane Grey,
and in trying to convert her to the doctrines of the
Catholic Church. Elizabeth loved flowers and she was
interdicted this pleasure. A child of one of the subor-
dinates of the constable was punished for presenting
her a bouquet, and the father of the child was igno-
miniously reprimanded. The chaplain of the Tower
came to instruct her in matters of religion; she dis-
sembled her real sentiments and heard the priest with
deference, and even attended mass with apparent
devotion, in order to take away all pretext for her
murder.

Among the many incidents that intensified the
estrangement of the two sisters was undoubtedly one
of deep-seated jealousy. The Queen had released the
Earl of Devonshire from his captivity, in which he
had passed the greater portion of his life, and touched
by his romantic misfortunes, and fascinated by the
beauty of his person, she had bestowed upon him as
much of her affections as a heart like hers could lavish
upon any one. But the Earl, while accepting her
gracious intentions, became suddenly smitten with the

more attractive graces of Elizabeth, and the Queen perceiving the change resented his infidelity as an indignity to her feelings and her honor.

Add to this the circumstance very generally believed that the great object of the Wyatt insurrection was to elevate Elizabeth to the throne, and to bring about her marriage with the Earl of Devonshire. It appears that they had been informed of the conspiracy; but this they denied, and they had so carefully guarded themselves that there was no material proof against them. The Earl was sent to Fotheringay, and then into exile, where he died. Elizabeth, as we have seen, was imprisoned in the Tower. It was determined at length to send her into the country, and an escort was provided to conduct her to the gloomy stronghold of Woodstock. Sir Henry Bedington was appointed to command the company. He was a rude soldier, more anxious to gratify his employers than to act as became his original station, so that he ranks among the jailors who have acquired infamy from the renown of their prisoners, and her treatment more than ever was still that of a criminal. When put into his charge she was unacquainted with his brutality, and although told that Woodstock was her destination she hardly trusted to the information. As they approached the exit from

the Tower, "Bedington," said she, in a husky under-
tone, with the piercing glance natural to her, "is the
Lady Jane's scaffold taken away?"

In aftertimes he presented himself at court; she
was contented with prohibiting his appearance there
in these stinging words, "God forgive you, and we do,
and if we have hereafter any prisoner whom we would
have hardly handled and strictly kept, then we will
send for you again." The remembrances of her own
misfortunes did not serve to soften the cruel wrongs
which she in her turn heaped upon Mary Stuart, in a
diabolical spirit of hatred and revenge that never drank
its wrathful cup to its dregs until she had signed the
death warrant for the execution of her imprisoned
victim.

Each new day brought to light an unsuspected
enemy. Even Wyatt, who had rushed headlong to
death, had been distinguished by her approbation of
his gallantry, accomplishments, and brilliant wit. He
was also a devout Catholic, the son and namesake of
the illustrious poet still read with delight in our own
generation. The elder Wyatt was a man of the most
gentle impulses, the soul of fidelity and deference to
high-born damsels. His sister Mary was the bosom
friend of Anne Boleyn, and gathered together her

remains on the scaffold. She and her brother transferred them by stealth and night to the family vault. He was Anne's biographer in the most touching of memorials. Yet this son had corrupted her armies, debauched her nobles, slain her guards before her palace, and ordered her to get married to some Englishman with as little ceremony as if she was a parish charge.

There were those to urge the execution of Jane Grey, as it was evident that she would be made the rallying point for every disturbance, as she had been in the rebellion just suppressed. They would not allow the melancholy girl locked up in the Tower to be unimpersonal, a dethroned Queen, and reproclaimed without her knowledge by her father, the Duke of Suffolk, and toasted as their future monarch by some of Wyatt's London allies. The very lords of the Council who had gone through the scene of Seymour's death, the execution of his brother, Somerset, and the decapitation of his successor, Northumberland, who had pronounced Mary illegitimate, and with the will of Edward in one hand and oaths of allegiance in the other had forced the crown upon her head, were now the most clamorous for her death. The deed was recommended to Mary in the field of blood before her palace; in the shock and horror of the moment she was told "such scenes would recur so long as she suffered a competitor for the throne to exist." It can only be said that she had an excuse denied to the stately and deliberate march of Elizabeth to the destruction of Mary Stuart.

Mary Tudor signed the death warrant of her kinswoman whilst the ground was slippery with blood around her door, when she had just escaped with life; when for the moment all hearts were hardened to bloodshed, for death and carnage surrounded them everywhere. It was never pretended by the authors of her untimely end that any principle but that of mere expediency demanded the execution of Lady Jane Grey. It was never maintained that she was in a moral and equitable sense a guilty person. The egregious overconfidence with which her father proclaimed her a second time brought its result upon her head; for she was no more accountable for his acts and intentions than she was for their failure. All the apologies of those in power were ethically on a par with the oriental economy of a seraglio. In a multiplicity of heirs public preferences are accommodated by narrowing the scope. The sovereign's twin-brother is strangled; a cousin with an indefeasible title is placed in a dungeon lower than the bottom of the Bosphorus ; a sprightly young nephew is kept from political mischief by searing his eyes with a red-hot iron.

One of these kinds of devices was proposed with regard to Lady Jane. The Emperor Charles recommended to his relative Mary a disposal of her cousin very much like immurement or being closed alive within a wall, like the iron cages in which Louis XI. left one of his Bishops to his reflections for ten years or more. The phrase used in his advisatory epistle is "*garder à vere*," and possesses no equivalent term in the more humane English language. It means substantially to be sealed from sight, to be passed into oblivion, as if in a mediæval *oubliette*. A pit among the corner stones of the Tower was conceived to be a convenient substitute should his advice be honored with the Queen's adoption. But even a fate so horrible as this was to contemplate would have scarcely appalled the soul within the quiet bosom, before which death presented no terrors.

In the history of Mary Tudor by Ernest Hemel he relates that one day Dr. Ascham came to the Tower, where Jane Grey was imprisoned, with a message from the Queen. She had been subjected to a rigorous

surveillance and confined to her apartment. This
inexorable sequestration had cost her much anxiety
and had become very painful. The object of Dr.
Ascham's visit was to inform her that henceforth she
would be permitted to promenade in the gardens of
the Tower. This good news made her very happy,
and she desired the doctor to express to the Queen her
warmest thanks for the favor.

This event occurred on one of the finest days of
returning springtime, and Jane immediately descended
from her place of confinement to respire the pure air
of which she had been deprived for the past three
months. There are moments in which the least little
corner of verdure appears like an enchanted spot;
the aspect of an unlimited horizon, the serenity of the
heavens, the verdant buds of the trees, the grass enam-
eled already with the first flowers, all these in the
beautiful gardens of the Tower penetrated the soul of
the pure young Queen with sweet consolations, and
again revived in her mind the hope of life.

At the moment when this visit took place the last
echoes of the Wyatt rebellion still resounded in the
country, and the execution of the sentence against her
had been resolved upon in the Council; Mary Tudor
resolved no longer to allow the existence of a rival

whose head for more than a week had worn the crown of England. The relaxation of rigor in the treatment of the gentle captive was only a prelude to the dreadful catastrophe of her death upon the scaffold. Ascham was charged at the same time with the cruel mission of announcing to Jane that she must prepare herself to die; but seeing her so serene and confident for the future, he knew not how to acquit himself of this sad mandate. While conversing with her about ancient authors and men who had been otherwise celebrated, they arrived at the banks of the Thames and seated themselves upon a bench near a little piece of woods. These trees, still deprived of their foliage, together with the monotonous murmur of the flowing waters in which the pale rays of the sun were reflected, inspired Jane with melancholy reflections. Then the aged doctor, taking her by the hands, thus addressed her: "Oh, my dear young Sovereign—for to me you are always the true Queen of this country—whatever may happen to me, who love you so much that they have confided to me the care of informing you of the destiny with which you are menaced"—here he was interrupted by his sobs and was unable to say more. Jane comprehended him perfectly, and received this terrible announcement with unaffected resignation. She

even consoled her devoted servitor and tried to support herself by the example of the illustrious person-
ages of antiquity.   Ascham instantly beseeched her to
take a poison that he had brought with him in order
that she might be spared the opprobrium and horror of
a public execution; she refused gently but firmly, saying that a Christian soul ought not voluntarily to take
his own life.

Whatever may have been the authority upon
which the author just named makes this statement,
certain it is that the solemn intelligence of her con-
demnation was communicated by Feckenham, the
Abbot of Westminster, and he very properly and naturally intimated to her the necessity of a preparation
for the awful change she was to undergo.

The zeal of Mary had, perhaps, falsely persuaded
her that conversion from a faith so considerately and
steadily entertained by Jane Grey could be effected at
the hour of death.   The chaplain used all those arguments so affecting and difficult to controvert from the
lips of piety and benevolence.   But her preparation
had long been made for an hour so constantly expected
and so little dreaded.   "A single day," she said, "was
a short time between the warning and death itself."
He hastened to the Queen and instantly procured a

respite. "The time was fearfully short," he said, "for preparation of any kind, and how could she expect the Lady Jane to die a Catholic if she were thus hurried to the block, without time for a conviction of her religious errors." But he had misunderstood the train of her thoughts; she only meant that one day was too short a time to compare conflicting opinions and impressions upon a subject so momentous; that it was the occupation of a lifetime, and her's were not the moments to enter upon a religious controversy. "But," she meekly added, "I am prepared to receive patiently my death in any manner it may please the Queen to appoint. It is true my frame shudders, as is natural to frail mortality; but my spirit will spring into the eternal light, where I trust the mercy of God will receive it." The Queen directed Feckenham to return to the Tower, having granted a respite of three days to discuss with her the truths of the Catholic belief. Jane Grey represented the circumstances in which she was placed, and which left her no time for a polemic discussion affecting her eternal welfare, and begged him to leave her alone to commune in solemn silence with her Maker, before whose throne she was so soon to appear; but Feckenham had invited two Bishops and two learned doctors to witness the dispute, and he

x.

was undoubtedly ambitious to display his powers before this noble and learned company. Jane finally consented to the interview.

Feckenham commenced as follows:

Feckenham.—Madam, I lament your heavy case, and yet I doubt not but that you bear out this heavy sorrow of yours with a constant and patient mind.

Lady Jane Grey.—You are welcome unto me, sir, if your coming be to give Christian exhortation. And as for my heavy case, I thank God I do so little lament it, that rather I account the same for a more manifest declaration of God's favor towards me than ever He showed me at any time before. And, therefore, there is no cause why either you or others, which bear me no good will, should lament or be grieved with this my case, being a thing so profitable for my soul's health.

F.—I am here come to you at this present time to instruct you in the true doctrine of the right faith; although I have so great confidence in you that I shall have, I trust, little need to travel with you much therein.

Jane.—Forsooth, I heartily thank the Queen's Highness, which is not unmindful of her humble subject; and I hope, likewise, that you no less will do your duty therein, both truly and faithfully, according to that you were sent for.

F.—What is then required of a Christian man?

Jane.—That he should believe in God the Father, the Son, and the Holy Ghost, three persons and one God.

F.—What, is there nothing else to be required or looked for in a Christian, but to believe in Him?

Jane.—Yes, we must love Him with all our heart, and all our soul, and with all our mind, and our neighbor as ourself.

F.—Why, then, faith neither justifieth nor saveth.

Jane.—Yes, verily, faith, as St. Paul saith, only justifieth.

F.—Why, St. Paul saith, If I have all faith without love, it is nothing.

Jane.—True it is; for how can I love him whom I trust not? Or how can I trust him whom I love not? Faith and love go both together, and yet love is comprehended in faith.

F.—How shall we love our neighbor?

Jane.—To love our neighbor is to feed the hungry, to clothe the naked, and give drink to the thirsty, and to do to him as we would do to ourselves.

F.—Why, then it is necessary unto salvation to do

good works also, and it is not sufficient only to believe.

Jane.—I deny that, and I affirm that faith only saveth; but it is meet for a Christian, in token that he followeth his Master Christ, to do good works, yet may we not say that they profit to our salvation. For when we have done all, yet we are unprofitable servants, and faith only in Christ's blood saveth us.

F.—How many sacraments are there?

Jane.—Two; the one the sacrament of baptism, and the other the sacrament of the Lord's supper.

F.—No, there are seven.

Jane.—By what scripture find you that?

F.—Well, we will talk of that hereafter. But what is signified by your two sacraments?

Jane.—By the sacrament of baptism I am washed with water, and regenerated by the Spirit, and that washing is a token to me that I am the child of God. The sacrament of the Lord's supper offered unto me is a sure seal and testimony that I am, by the blood of Christ, which He shed for me on the cross, made partaker of the everlasting kingdom.

F.—Why, what do you receive in that sacrament? Do you not receive the very body and blood of Christ?

Jane.—No, surely, I do not so believe. I think that at the supper I neither receive flesh nor blood, but bread and wine; which bread, when it is broken, and the wine, when it is drank, putteth me in remembrance how that for my sins the body of Christ was broken, and His blood shed on the cross, and with that bread and wine I receive the benefits that come by the breaking of His body and the shedding of His blood for our sins on the cross.

F.—Why, doth not Christ speak these words: Take, eat; this is my body? Require you any plainer words? Doth He not say it is His body?

Jane.—I grant He saith so; and so He saith, I am the vine, I am the door; but He is never the more the door nor the vine. Doth not St. Paul say, He calleth things that are not, as though they were? God forbid that I should say that I eat the very natural body and blood of Christ; for then, either I should pluck away my redemption, or else there were two bodies, or two Christs. One body was tormented on the cross, and if they did eat another body, then had He two bodies; or, if His body were eaten, then it was not broken upon the cross, or if it were broken upon the cross, it was not eaten of His disciples.

F.—Why? Is it not as possible that Christ, by His power, could make His body both to be eaten and broken, as to be born of a woman without seed of man, and to walk upon the sea, having a body, and other such like miracles as He wrought by His power only?

Jane.—Yes, verily, if God would have done at His supper any miracles, He might have done so; but I say, that when He minded no work nor miracles, but only to break His body, and shed His blood on the cross for our sins. But I pray you to answer me this one question. Where was Christ when He said, Take, eat; this is my body? Was He not at the table when He said so? He was at that time alive, and suffered not till the next day. What took He but bread? what brake He but bread? and what gave He but bread? Look, what He took He brake; and look, what He brake He gave; and look, what He gave, they did eat; and yet all this while He Himself was alive, and at supper before His disciples; or else they were deceived.

F.—You ground your faith upon such authors as say and unsay both in a breath, and not upon the church, to whom you ought to give credit.

Jane.—No, I ground my faith on God's word, and not upon the church; for if the church be a good church, the faith of the church must be tried by God's word, and not God's word by the church, nor yet my faith. Shall I believe the church because of antiquity? or shall I give credit to the church that taketh away from me the half part of the Lord's supper, and will not let any man receive it in both kinds? which things, if they deny to us, then deny they to us a part of our salvation. And I say that it is an evil church, and not the spouse of Christ, but the spouse of the devil that altereth the Lord's supper, and both taketh from it and addeth to it. To that church (say I) God will add plagues, and from that church will He take their part out of the book of life. Do they learn that of St. Paul, when he ministered to the Corinthians in both kinds? Shall I believe this church? God forbid.

F.—That was done for a good intent of the church to avoid an heresy that sprang up from it.

Jane.—Why? shall the church alter God's will and ordinance for good intent? How did King Saul? The Lord God defend.

The conversation proceeded in like manner, but to no purpose. When Feckenham took his leave he said:

F.—I am sorry for you; for I am sure that we two shall never more meet.

Jane.—True it is, that we shall never meet, except God turn your heart. For I am assured unless you repent and turn to God, you are in an evil case; and I pray God, in the bowels of His mercy, to send you His Holy Spirit; for He hath given you His great gift of utterance, if it pleased Him also to open the eyes of your heart.

Throughout the whole discussion Lady Jane conducted herself with the utmost calmness and meekness; indeed her witnesses were astonished at her deportment, as well as by her vigor of mind and language. She has left somewhere among her books, the following lines in reference to this discussion:

" Mr. Feckenham gave me a long, tedious, yet eloquent reply, using many strong and logical persuasions to compel me to have leaned to their church; but my faith hath armed my resolution to withstand any assault that words could then use against me. Of many other articles of religion we reasoned; but those formerly rehearsed were the chiefest and most effectual.

"JANE DUDLEY."

I doubt if there is a more surprising example of mental acumen to be found anywhere in general history. With nothing but her own resources, unskilled in the technicalities of disputations, defenseless and alone; she had been a prisoner for six months, her blood chilled by confinement, her heart blanched with sorrow, without counsel, consultation, or the means of preparation; the shadow of the scaffold resting upon her fair and fragile form, and with a horrible

death to occur in a few hours; she met this array of
learning, ability, and power, confounding her judges
with the simple truth of her convictions. Her last
hours were devoted to prayer and writing the last fare-
wells on earth to her friends and family. To Harding,
whose friendship she prized, and whose apostacy she
deplored, she wrote a long and ardent appeal. She
felt that standing disenthralled from all earthly hopes
and interests, he might listen to a voice from the verge
of two existences, and if insincerely renouncing his
faith, be brought to a deeper reflection by the solemnity
of the circumstances under which she addressed him.
On the blank leaves of a Greek Testament she sent to
her sister Catherine as a last memorial, she wrote in
the same language a letter exhorting her to be steadfast in her faith, to live prepared to suffer the fate that
the will of Heaven had reserved for herself.

No trait was ever elicited by life or death from the
conduct of a human being more beautiful and glorious
in its filial piety than her dying letter to the father
who had from the first to the last undesignedly, but
still unvaryingly, brought her to a violent death. She
does not seem to be aware of his constant instrumen-
tality in her misfortunes. It appears that in her eyes
to the existence of such a daughter is alone attributable

the grief and desolation that invaded their family hearth, and while protesting her innocence of intentional wrong, she prays that her own sacrifice may shield others from suffering who are also innocent. She exclaims, "My guiltless blood may cry before the Lord, mercy to the innocent."

The following is a copy of a letter from Lady Jane to her father:

" FATHER :—

"Although it hath pleased God to hasten my death by you, by whom my life should rather have been lengthened, yet can I so patiently take it, as yield more hearty thanks for shortening my woful days, than if the whole world had been given unto my possession, with life lengthened at my own will. And albeit I am well assured of your impatient griefs, redoubled manifold ways, both in bewailing your own woe, and especially, as I hear, my unfortunate state ; yet my dear father, if I may without offence rejoice in my own mishaps, meseems in this I may account myself blessed, that washing my hands in the innocency of my fact, my guiltless blood may cry before the Lord, mercy to the innocent. And yet though I must needs acknowledge, that being constrained, and as you wot well enough, continually assayed, in taking upon me I seemed to consent, and therein grievously offended the Queen and her laws ; yet do I assuredly trust, that this my offence towards God is so much the less, in that being in so royal estate as I was, my enforced honor blended never with mine innocent heart ; and thus, good father, I have opened unto you the state wherein I at present stand. Whose death at hand, although to you, perhaps, it may seem right woful, to me there is nothing that can be more welcome, than from this vale of misery to aspire to that heavenly throne of all joy and pleasure, with Christ our Saviour. In whose steadfast faith, if it may be lawful for the daughter so to write to the father, the Lord that hitherto hath strengthened you, so continue you, that at the last we may meet in heaven with the Father, the Son, and the Holy Ghost.   JANE."

The time of the respite wore on. The nearness of the fatal hour elevated instead of depressing the equanimity of her thoughts and the sublimity of her conversation. It had been intended that her husband and herself should be placed together on the same scaffold, and executed in each other's sight. For this purpose it was erected on Tower Hill. Before the hour arrived, however, it was apprehended that such an attachment as the people now testified to the condemned might assume an expression dangerous to the peace of the city, if not, indeed, to render the fulfillment of the law impossible.

The populace, inebriated as they were with judicial murders since they could walk, had never beheld a scene so agonizing as shedding the blood of so much youth, innocence, and personal beauty for an involuntary usurpation; neither of the victims was over seventeen years old, and they were husband and wife. It seemed the wanton revel of massacre to take their young lives—the boy, so noble in his air, so slender and beardless ; and she, beautiful being, last mid-summer's day was their Queen.

When it was determined to execute them separately, and it was impossible to bid each other farewell on the scaffold, Dudley desired permission to see her before they died. She heroically denied them both the last embrace the world could witness. The parting, she said, would unnerve the firmness with which death should be met; that their fortitude could not be regained in an instant; but that the separation would be but for a moment, and their reunion eternal, where misfortune and crime would no more disturb their eternal felicity.

There is a picture of the instant when she looked out of her prison window and beheld the body of her husband brought headless from Tower Hill, in which the furniture, as then it existed, her books yet preserved, and her name on the wall yet unerased, struck me as one of the most melancholy and depressing efforts of art that I ever looked upon. This simplicity is, perhaps, the field in which the fancy ranges to supply all the sad incidents of which we have read. They had told her of the constancy with which her husband met his fate, and as she was blessing Heaven that his pain was over a low signal warned her that death had come to lead her the way. She covered herself with a mantle of fur, for the weather was bitterly cold, and passed through the solemn ranks that guided her to the doomsman. The old constable of the Tower asked her for a token to keep in perpetual remembrance; she gave him a note-book in which she had just written three sentences, one in Greek, one in Latin, and one in English. Of her husband she said human justice had wronged his body, but Divine mercy would show favor to his soul; with regard to herself the words were, "If my fault deserved punishment, my youth, at least, and my imprudence were worthy of excuse, and God and posterity, I trust, will show me favor."

The platform was erected within the enclosure of the Tower. Before she unrobed she spoke clearly and without hesitation to those admitted, for the sympathy of the populace had caused their exclusion. Her mild, self-denying disposition inclined her to ward off all blame from others. She said her offence was not in assuming the crown, but in not rejecting it with sufficient constancy; that she had less erred through ambition than through reverence to her parents; that she willingly received her death as the only atonement she could now make to the injured state. And although her act was committed under constraint, she willingly offered her life to the offended laws, and gave them all left to her—a voluntary submission; that her soul was as pure from trespass against Queen Mary as innocence was from injustice, for, said she, "I only consented to the deed I was forced into." Then taking Feckenham by the hand, she thanked him for the many good offices she had received from him and recognized the goodness of his motives, and said that she had no apprehension of what she was about to suffer; then looking around with a placid countenance on the crowd, she bade them farewell and asked them to remember her innocence. Then kneeling down before the axe and covering her face with her hair, she received the stroke that severed her head from her body. The sighs and sobs, the tears and moans, and the mournful words of the beholders testified what their feelings were concerning the circumstances of her death and the saintlike and steady manner with which she had submitted to an end so tragical and sad.

When we reflect upon the circumstances that led to the sacrifice of this untarnished life—the fairest, wisest, and most brilliant descendant in the realm from the house of Lancaster—we cannot but feel that a step of the simplest innocence, taken under constraint, was sought as a pretext for shedding her blood. Called from the exercise of unnumbered virtues, and from the cultivation of her mind and the elevated bent of its pursuits, she humbly acquiesced when called to the crown, and submitted to lay it down as modestly as she had taken it up. Could a character so unblemished by ambition, so amiable, so modest, and so prematurely wise, consent to a measure that ought to be revenged as a usurpation, and that could form a successful excuse for mercilessly putting her to death? She fell a victim to the clamor of hearts of stone and an insensate rage for shedding the best blood in the land, but the spell of her character, the beauty of her life have encircled her name with a lustre that has been diffused to the present day.

THE END.

ERRATA.

In seventh line of page 95, instead of Dundee read Arundel.

In third line of page 103, instead of Suffolk read Norfolk.

Made in the USA
Middletown, DE
03 August 2023

36063698R00104